# BEYOND Implicit & Explicit BIAS

## Strategies for Healing the Root Causes of Inequity in EDUCATION

## ClauDean ChiNaka Kizart

Solution Tree | Press

555 North Morton Street
Bloomington, IN 47404
800.733.6786 (toll free) / 812.336.7700
FAX: 812.336.7790
email: info@SolutionTree.com
SolutionTree.com

Visit **go.SolutionTree.com/diversityandequity** to download the free reproducibles in this book.

Printed in the United States of America

Library of Congress Cataloging-in-Publication Data

Names: Kizart, ClauDean ChiNaka, author.
Title: Beyond implicit and explicit bias : strategies for healing the root
  causes of inequity in education / ClauDean ChiNaka Kizart.
Description: Bloomington, IN : Solution Tree Press, 2024. | Includes
  bibliographical references and index.
Identifiers: LCCN 2024030688 (print) | LCCN 2024030689 (ebook) | ISBN
  9781954631618 (paperback) | ISBN 9781954631625 (ebook)
Subjects: LCSH: Educational equalization--United States. | Discrimination
  in education--United States. | Teaching--United States--Psychological
  aspects. | Teachers--United States--Attitudes.
Classification: LCC LC213.2 .K59 2024  (print) | LCC LC213.2  (ebook) | DDC
  379.2/60973--dc23/eng/20240913
LC record available at https://lccn.loc.gov/2024030688
LC ebook record available at https://lccn.loc.gov/2024030689

**Solution Tree**
Jeffrey C. Jones, CEO
Edmund M. Ackerman, President

**Solution Tree Press**
*President and Publisher:* Douglas M. Rife
*Associate Publishers:* Todd Brakke and Kendra Slayton
*Editorial Director:* Laurel Hecker
*Art Director:* Rian Anderson
*Copy Chief:* Jessi Finn
*Senior Production Editor:* Christine Hood
*Copy Editor:* Charlotte Jones
*Text and Cover Designer:* Kelsey Hoover
*Acquisitions Editors:* Carol Collins and Hilary Goff
*Content Development Specialist:* Amy Rubenstein
*Associate Editors:* Sarah Ludwig and Elijah Oates
*Editorial Assistant:* Anne Marie Watkins

# Dedication

*Art is powerful, art is important, art can change hearts and minds all the way across the world.*

—R. Alan Brooks

To me writing is art . . . paper is my canvas. I dedicate this book of art to all well-intentioned educators, board members, administrators, pre-service teachers, consultants, and others who are interested in improving our communities, nation, and world through education. To my ancestors, parents, grandparents, children, and civil rights leaders of all races, creeds, and colors who fought for equal access to education. To those of us who work to carry the torch further so that there is equity in education.

# Acknowledgments

give thanks to the spirit from which love originates and flows. I am deeply grateful for my ancestors, including my father, William Edgar Anderson; Paw Paw Stout Kizart Jr.; Grandma Hoover C. Kizart; Mamie Lee Sylvester; Jugeirtha Sylvester; my friend and forever bonus father in spirit, Dan Bogaty; as well as all the Andersons, Kizarts, Parkers, Rollins, Hawthorns, and Grimes. To all those ancestors whose names I did not mention or do not know, thank you. To my Black, White, Native American, and Congolese ancestors—had it not been for you, I would not be.

To my mother, Creola Kizart Hampton, and her husband, Levant G. Hampton, thank you for raising me well. Deep appreciation to my sisters, Dr. Camille Kizart-Clark and Cosette L. Hampton-Ayele, as well as my two amazing children, Destinae and Jeremie Lindor, who often asked, "Mommy, how is your book going?" You two are something special! I am lucky to be your mom. Auntie Mamie, Uncle Antwine, Uncle Clay, Auntie Barbara Ann, Uncle Blaze, and all my cousins, I love y'all! Your presence reminds me of the importance of unity, the beauty of family, and the grace of forgiveness.

To my godmother, Inetta Johnson, thank you for seeing beauty in me when many others only saw scars. Ma B (Vanessa Bogaty) and Dr. Iya Asabi Thomas-Mosley, my two bonus mothers, thank you for keeping me from "twirling" and providing years of advice that I carry with me more than you know. Pat Johnson; Cortez L. Battle; Veronica Banks; Pat Johnson; Auntie Dr. Michelle Ellis-Young; Barbara Hamm Lee; Janice Anderson; John Waters; Sheri Kulpa; Dr. Marsha Conston; Curt Aasen;

Dr. Michelle Woodhouse; Baba Alaje Thomas; Baba Darrick Griffin; Iya Tiombe Meteye; Amy Rubenstein; Iya Josephine Williams; Iya Zola Mashariki; Dr. Iya Sauda Smith; Dr. Jamille Edwards, my writing accountability partner; and everyone who has and continues to provide mentorship . . . thank you! Adupe!

To the host of students who continue to reach out and remind me of the positive impact I've made in your lives—this book is for you, your children, your children's children, and all those educators who will make a positive impact in their lives as well.

Solution Tree Press would like to thank the following reviewers:

Taylor Bronowicz
Sixth-Grade Mathematics Teacher
Albertville Intermediate School
Albertville, Alabama

Erin Kruckenberg
Fifth-Grade Teacher
Jefferson Elementary School
Harvard, Illinois

Courtney Burdick
Apprenticeship Mentor Teacher
Fort Smith Public Schools
Fort Smith, Arkansas

Vanessa Cevallos Reyes
Principal
Sam Rayburn High School
Pasadena, Texas

Carrie Cutler
Clinical Associate Professor
University of Houston
Houston, Texas

Janel Ross
Principal
White River School District
Buckley, Washington

Janet Gilbert
Principal
Mountain Shadows Elementary School
Glendale, Arizona

Lauren Smith
Instructional Coach
Noble Crossing Elementary School
Noblesville Schools
Noblesville, Indiana

Kelly Hilliard
GATE Mathematics Instructor NBCT
Darrell C. Swope Middle School
Reno, Nevada

Rosemarie Nodine Swallow
Social Studies Teacher
Lava Ridge Intermediate
Santa Clara, Utah

Teresa Kinley
Humanities Teacher
Calgary, Alberta, Canada

Visit **go.SolutionTree.com/diversityandequity** to download the free reproducibles in this book.

# Table of Contents

*Reproducibles are in italics.*

## CHAPTER 2
## Dunning-Kruger Effect Bias . . . . . . . . . . . . . . . . . . . . . . . . . . . 35

## CHAPTER 3
## Herd Mentality Bias . . . . . . . . . . . . . . . . . . . . . . . . . . . . . . . . . . . 55

## CHAPTER 4
## Anchoring Bias . . . . . . . . . . . . . . . . . . . . . . . . . . . . . . . . . . . . . . . . 71

# About the Author

**ClauDean ChiNaka Kizart, EdD,** is a distinguished diversity, equity, and inclusion-certified leader with more than twenty-five years of experience in grades K–12 and higher education. She is widely known for her ability to inspire positive change within diverse communities. Currently, she serves as the Institutional Director of Diversity, Equity, and Inclusion at a community college. As a professional development facilitator, she provides data-informed solutions that result in positive impact, especially in the areas of diversity, equity, inclusion, belonging, and accessibility in education.

Having worked with both urban and rural communities, her approach is rooted in the belief that education is a pathway to empowerment and that unity strengthens all communities. As a respected educator, administrator, and facilitator of equity-driven professional development, Dr. Kizart regularly leads training focused on honoring diversity, cultivating a more inclusive school community, creating equitable educational environments, and other topics at conferences, including Write to Learn, Learning Forward, YMCA R.E.S.T, and GlobalMindED.

Her dissertation, *The Challenges of Persisting First Generation College Students*, has been widely cited and contributed to the Pell Institute's Study of Opportunity in Education. Dr. Kizart is also a member of several state and national organizations, including the National Association of Diversity Officers in Higher Education,

Virginia Center for Inclusive Communities (VCIC), Virginia Association of Diversity Officers in Higher Education, and Virginia Organization for Inclusive Concepts and Equitable Solutions (VOICES). She has been awarded the Outstanding Faculty and Service Award at St. Louis Community College, as well as the Betts Outstanding Teacher Award.

She received her bachelor's degree in elementary education from Harris-Stowe State University, lifetime reading certification from Fontbonne University, master's degree in educational administration from Saint Louis University, and a doctorate in educational leadership from Lindenwood University.

A native of Chicago and mother of two, Dr. Kizart's educational career spans roles as a special education teacher, literacy coach, middle school educator, and statewide equity trainer. As a lover of African-Caribbean traditions, Dr. Kizart brings a rich cultural perspective rooted in love to her work in diversity, equity, and inclusion (DEI).

To learn more about Dr. Kizart's work, follow her @Dr. ClauDean Kizart on LinkedIn or @DocKizart on Instagram.

To book ClauDean ChiNaka Kizart for professional development, contact pd@Solution Tree.com.

# Introduction

*We want to discover and unearth our biases and then allow ourselves a lot of grace.*

—Claudia Wheatley

There is an African proverb that states, "When two elephants fight, it is the grass that suffers." I am an elephant. When I began my work as an educator, it did not take long for me to recognize I was not fully prepared for the labor of love it took to teach literacy to an entire class of more than twenty-five students. Like many teachers, I started teaching fresh out of college. I was full of ideas, lesson plans, thematic units, and excitement. My excitement was met with a class of fifth-grade students who read on various grade levels. Some were reading above or on grade level, while the majority were reading significantly below grade level. The "grass" (or students) was suffering. Because I graduated from a university that taught me to be a reflective educator, every day after school, I asked myself three questions.

1. What did I teach well today?

2. How could I have done better?

3. What will I do differently tomorrow?

As I drove home after school every day, I reflected on these questions and considered the academic and social engagement of all my students. I learned to celebrate every "aha" moment and find solutions to every "oh my" moment. The aha moments were light bulbs—ideas and lessons I thought went well. The oh my moments were also light bulbs, indicating I needed to do something differently. Both were based on student engagement and performance. It was not enough that I felt good about the lessons and social engagement of my students; what mattered most was that they "got it."

During my first month or two of teaching, I noticed many students did not, in fact, get it. The main "it" they did not get was reading. As an educator, I felt responsible. Coming from a family of educators, I knew it was my responsibility to study materials in and out of the classroom setting and find ways to meet the needs of students no matter what race, ethnicity, socioeconomic status, reading level, gender, religious belief, sexual orientation, or any other difference. I learned that good educators reach outside of their personal biases and seek community resources when necessary to help their students excel. Additionally, good educators know that beyond the politics surrounding the words *equity* and *inclusion*, the work of honoring the diversity of school communities by furthering our knowledge of biases, as well as how to manage them, is important.

Whether your school is in a state experiencing politics around these issues, educators need to be sure they aren't making biased decisions that affect school communities. For example, during a professional development session I facilitated titled "Check Your Bias," a participant shared a concern that many students in her high school class did not want to engage in conversations related to race. As a White woman who struggled with conversations about race, she was reaching out for solutions to help open the dialogue in her ethnically diverse classroom. She wanted to engage students in conversations about race related to a piece of literature they were required to read. During our conversation, she stated, "I don't agree with all that DEI, EDI, DEIJA stuff, but as a White woman, I just don't know how to engage my students in a way that won't make them feel bad."

She was open to bringing in an outside person to help facilitate the conversation. To her, the most important thing was her students and their ability to grow through dialogue. She wanted them to "get it"! She was an example of an educator who acknowledged her own bias and sought guidance to educate her students. Similarly, as a teacher, I felt responsible for addressing the gaps I was seeing in my students' learning. This quest led me back to college.

I went back to school to complete my master's degree in educational administration and became a certified reading specialist. My goal was to gather the tools necessary to assist students on, above, or below grade level in reading. This goal was rooted in *equity*, not equality. It was not enough to give all my students the same reading material and expect them to get it. My students needed to develop the skills to be fluent readers with greater opportunities for college and career advancement.

As a first-year teacher, I developed what I now know as *equity consciousness,* a term first coined by Linda E. Skrla, Kathyrn B. McKenzie, and James J. Scheurich in 2009. Equity consciousness is centered on four essential beliefs.

1. All children (except only a small percentage, e.g., those with profound disabilities) are capable of elevated levels of academic success.
2. *All* children means *all*, regardless of a child's race, social class, gender, sexual orientation, learning differences, culture, language, and so on.
3. The adults in school are primarily responsible for student learning.
4. Traditional school practices may work for some students but are not working for all students. Therefore, if we are going to eliminate the achievement gap, it requires a change in practice (pp. 12–13).

As a professional educator, I believed (and still do) that as an "elephant," it is my vocational responsibility to nurture all "shards of grass"—the tall ones, the short ones, and all those in between. Anthony Muhammad and Luiz F. Cruz (2019), two of the most influential educators and authors in the field of education, discuss the importance of our responsibility as educators to transform the lives of students through significantly impacting student outcomes. How we impact the students' lives heavily relies on our ability as educators to be transformational leaders who understand that our behavior "significantly contributes to schools, districts, families, communities, and world" (Muhammad & Cruz, 2019, p. 5).

> The quest to empower and transform students' lives cannot be a game of chance.

The quest to empower and transform students' lives cannot be a game of chance. Knowledge and intentional work to unearth biases that lead to harmful actions which counteract the work of improving our school communities is undoubtedly an essential quality of all educators. Regularly addressing and leveraging proactive solutions to counteract our biases as educators helps to facilitate changes needed to close gaps in equity.

A lot of well-intentioned people are great educators. Many of us are beginning to examine blind spots, bias, culture, White privilege, and diversity, equity, and inclusion (DEI). Discussing, formulating, and leveraging solutions to the ailments which negatively impact our students, especially issues related to DEI, are front and center.

Due to federal laws, many states and local districts are required to submit equity plans. Acknowledging inequity in schools is a good step; however, without taking a deeper look and developing strategies to heal the root causes of inequity, I am concerned that we may fail in our well-intentioned endeavors to create equity.

If we were to compare educators to gardeners, one might say that, like gardeners, we have a moral and professional obligation to provide the most fertile ground for students to cultivate their intellectual and social abilities. Gardeners monitor the health of all plants, flowers, and green spaces. Gardeners water, feed, weed, and trim trees and shrubs while also fertilizing and keeping beautiful green spaces and walkways clear of debris. Gardeners, like educators, are busy. They do not just have one task ahead of them each day. When there are problems with a tree or leaves of a plant, one of the first things a gardener will do is examine the roots. Often, roots need to be treated so trees and other plants flourish. To this point, this book examines the roots of inequity and offers treatments in the form of reflection questions, scenarios, equity checklists, and other tools for cultivating healthier roots in our collective quest to provide more equitable education for students around the world. With this in mind, the purpose of this book is threefold.

1. It deepens understanding of specific biases that cause inequities in school communities. There is a large body of research exploring implicit and explicit biases. It is my hope this book will help you move from a general to specific understanding of biases you can relate to and counteract.

2. It provides school-based scenarios and opportunities for reflection to support readers in "checking" their biases on the journey to systemic equity in schools.

3. It shares specific strategies and tips to recognize specific biases, examine their roots, explore the impact they have on the school community, and learn strategies to counteract biases to cultivate school communities where the sense of belonginess is so strong that students will *want* to come to school every day.

As you read this book, I encourage you to be objective. See yourself, but don't be ashamed of yourself or anyone else. Approach every chapter from a space of curiosity and openness to be a better educator. As educators, our communities and the world are depending on us to create more inclusive school communities that honor diverse perspectives, backgrounds, ethnicity, race, gender, religion, abilities, sexual orientation, and so on. That work begins with learning more about specific biases that cause even the most well-intentioned educator to make decisions counter to their values, best practices, and quality education for all students.

Managing our biases, while also assisting students and others within our school communities, is not always easy. We must be willing to see ourselves, reflect, self-correct, and move forward with love. My mother taught me that *love* is an action word. Additionally, knowing the root or the "why" helps encourage us to keep moving forward during challenging times. In an increasingly diverse society, remembering why we decided to work in the field of education, while using the strategies in this book to manage our biases, is a great way of putting our love for education and our love for students into action.

> *Love* is an action word.

# Why Now

During the height of the COVID-19 pandemic, I created a campaign called "Remembering My Why" for a professional development agency. I wanted to encourage teachers to remember, during an enormously tumultuous time, why they began teaching. Remembering our why inspires us during some of our darkest moments. Remembering our why keeps us moving forward when we would not otherwise or when things are challenging, and we want to give up.

> Remembering our why inspires us during some of our darkest moments.

While drafting this book, I wanted to give up many times. There were times I thought, do I have anything significant to say? Do I have anything important to say that has not already been said? Is there space for my book? Will people read this book? It is in these moments I remembered my why. My *professional why* is to share information that will empower people, especially educators who will assist in cultivating equitable and inclusive spaces where everyone thrives. My *personal why* is grounded in the belief that everyone is worthy of being seen, valued, heard, and well educated. This is especially important as racial and ethnic demographics shift.

According to the 2010 and 2020 census data from the U.S. Census Bureau, the ethnic and racial composition of the United States is shifting considerably (U.S. Census Bureau, 2010, 2020, 2021). Comparable data from these two censuses revealed the following.

- The multiracial population increased from 9 million to 33.8 million people between 2010 and 2020, which is a 276 percent increase.

- The White population remained the largest race or ethnic group in 2020, with a reported 235.4 million identifying as White or in combination with other groups; however, this is an 8.6 percent decrease from the 2010 census for this racial demographic in the United States.

- The U.S. population of Blacks or African Americans increased from 39.0 million to 41.1 million, which is an 11.7 percent increase between 2010 and 2020.

- The Asian population increased from 14.7 million people to 19.9 million, between 2010 and 2020. This represents a 35 percent growth of the Asian population.

- The American Indian and Alaska Native population in the United States increased from 2.9 million in 2010 to 3.7 million in 2020, representing a 85.2 percent population growth.

- The Native Hawaiian and Other Pacific Islander population increased from 540,013 in 2010 to 689,966 in 2020, which represents a 29.5 percent increase of this demographic.

- The Latinx population, which includes Mexican, Hispanic, Latin American, and Puerto Rican ethnic groups, increased from 3 million to 20.3 million. This represents a 567 percent increase in this population.

Additionally, according to the Pew Research Center (2020), Generation Z, those born between 1997 and 2012, is more ethnically diverse than former generations.

This is largely due to the growing population of interracial, biracial, Hispanic, Latinx, Black, and Asian people in the United States.

Another growing demographic to consider as we cultivate systemic equity and inclusion in our school communities is the increased population of the LGBTQ+ community, which includes but is not limited to lesbian, gay, bisexual, transgender women, transgender men, two-spirited, queer, intersex, questioning, nonbinary, asexual, and other identities outside of the heterosexual criterion (Goldberg, Rothblum, Russell, & Meyer, 2020; Human Rights Campaign, 2021).

According to a 2024 poll by Gallup, a global analytic and advice firm, an estimated 7.6 percent of adults identify as LGBTQ+ or something other than heterosexual. This percentage has more than doubled since the initial poll in 2012 (Gallup, 2012, 2024). In July of 2021, the U.S. Census Bureau's Household Pulse Survey began to include sexual orientation and gender identity in the questionnaire, which aims to gain a more comprehensive understanding of the LGBTQ+ population in the United States (U.S. Census Bureau, n.d.).

Considering statistics regarding the changing demographics, particularly in the United States, it has become increasingly important that we stop going along to get along. Although Black and Indigenous people of color legally have the equal opportunity to teach, lead, and study anywhere they want, are those opportunities and spaces equitable? Are educational structures safe for people to be different? Do educational systems intentionally make room for everyone to achieve? Do people truly understand that their biases often undermine the good work they say they want to do, their policies and procedures, and the way that they interact with other educators and administrators, as well as students? This book provides clarity about the biases that undermine good intentions, as well as the policies, practices, and behaviors that govern people's thoughts and, therefore, our schools.

Early in my teaching career, I had the pleasure of facilitating instruction in a classroom full of skill builders. Skill builders are students who challenge and stretch you to build the skills of patience, compassion, organization, and adaptability. As I reflected on why this book and why now, a few of those skill builders came to mind. There was one student in my fifth-grade class who was extremely talented. He was one of those students who was quick-witted and finished his work before everyone else. His penmanship was outstanding; he was a mathematical genius; and even when I thought he was not listening during small-group reading time, he was able to answer every comprehension question with fidelity. He also had an amazingly bad temper. Unfortunately, his inability to navigate through his emotions in a healthy way was often the only thing teachers made comments about during our team meetings.

It was widely known in the school that he and his siblings, whom we called the "Smith kids," were more than just skill builders; they were troublemakers. One day, while I was in the teachers' lounge, a teacher made an interesting comment about one of the Smith kids. She said, "I already have a seat reserved for him at the front of the room, so when he starts to act out, he doesn't impact the rest of the class or keep others from learning." There was something about that comment that did not sit well with me. The mere notion that behavioral issues superseded the intellectual abilities of the Smith kids was damaging to the type of inclusive school communities we strive to create.

The fact that I did not have the courage to speak up is something I still deeply regret. I was a new teacher who came to the teacher's lounge hoping to build camaraderie and didn't feel comfortable enough to say anything. However, after hearing one too many flagrantly biased comments about students, I simply stopped eating in the teachers' lounge. I still remember the fear of speaking up and the fear of being treated differently if I did.

It is for the Smith kids and many others that I write this book. Over the course of twenty-five years of being an educator, I have heard many biased comments made by a wide variety of people, including teachers, administrators, and other school leaders. Often, these comments were made by very well-intentioned educators whose deep-rooted biases impacted the most innocent of us all . . . our students.

For the first few years I served as a classroom teacher, I said nothing when I heard harmful and stereotypical comments made about students. I know now that I struggled with herd mentality bias (discussed in chapter 3, page 55). Rather than go against the group (or herd), I did something that the book *Crucial Conversations* (Patterson, Grenny, McMillian, & Switzler, 2012) discusses as one of the three ways people handle critical conversations . . . I avoided them.

# Terms and Definitions

Being aware of specific biases and learning how to counteract them are essential to creating communities where everyone is truly embraced and can flourish. Not being aware of specific biases and how they cause us to make harmful decisions can negatively impact the students we serve. First, it's important to understand the terms related to bias, equity, and diversity.

In his book *The Emotional Brain: The Mysterious Underpinnings of Emotional Life*, neuroscientist Joseph LeDoux (1998) explains that our biases cause us to make assumptions before we have a chance to cognitively consider our actions. Our biases impact the way we make decisions. Therefore, it is important to move from general to specific knowledge about the various types of biases that cause harm in educational communities. This book is your key to building knowledge about specific biases, understanding how they impact schools, and learning essential strategies to help you counteract the negative impact of bias.

> Our biases impact the way we make decisions.

It is important to understand how I define *equity*, *inclusion*, and other important terms in this book. Although a clear definition of *equity* would seem necessary to move the needle to cultivate systemic equity into action, the field of education is just beginning to explore what it really means. Therefore, for the purpose of this book, I will use the following definitions to ensure a shared understanding of these terms.

- **Equity:** The National Equity Project defines *equity* as ensuring each person receives what they need to develop to their academic and social potential. School equity involves interrupting inequitable practices, examining biases, and creating inclusive multicultural school environments for adults and children (National Equity Project, 2024).

- **Bias:** Bias is a disproportionate weight in favor of or against an idea or thing, usually in a way that is closed-minded, prejudicial, or unfair. Biases can be innate or learned. People may develop biases for or against an individual, a group, or a belief. In science and engineering, bias is a systematic error. Merriam-Webster defines *bias* as follows: "(1) an inclination of temperament or outlook, *especially* a personal and sometimes unreasoned judgment; (2) an instance of such prejudice; or (3) a systematic error introduced into sampling or testing by selecting or encouraging one outcome or answer over another" (Bias, n.d.).

- **Diverse:** This term encompasses the width and breadth of identities and backgrounds among various populations, which includes socioeconomic, ethnic, linguistic, and geographic self-reported identity markers as well as gender, sexual orientation, age, disability, nationality, migrant status, homelessness, educational status, undocumented status, and neurodiversity, which refers to the range of differences in brain function.

- **Explicit bias:** This is a conscious awareness of beliefs, attitudes, and actions that are often formed through our upbringing, societal influences, lived experiences, exposure to media, and other interactions. Explicit biases are based on conscious beliefs about gender, age, religion, race, ethnicity, sexual orientation, socioeconomic abilities or disabilities, level of education, weight, appearance, and other characteristics. Explicit biases are usually leveled at a group of people directly or through "coded" language that can be deduced through inference and changed through education and self-reflection (Banaji & Greenwald, 1995; Boysen & Vogel, 2009).

- **Implicit bias:** This is an unconscious belief, attitude, stereotype, reaction, or assumption that affects behavior and can significantly impact decision making, often without awareness. Implicit bias can fuel the automatic reactions we have toward other people, which can negatively impact our understanding, actions, and decision making. These implicit or unconscious biases impact various aspects of society, including education, as well as organizational practices like hiring and promotion (Banaji & Greenwald, 1995; Boysen & Vogel, 2009).

- **Inclusion:** This term refers to attitudes, behaviors, and methods that ensure individuals can bring their "whole selves" and fully participate in every aspect of society, including education (Winters, 2013). In a 2014 report, the United Nations International Children's Emergency Fund (UNICEF) described inclusion as a "universal human right" needed to embrace and show value for everyone irrespective of race, gender, disability, ethnicity, sexual orientation, age, and so on (UNICEF, 2017).

- **Belongingness:** This is a universal need to be part of a group through forming positive and stable interpersonal relationships. Research by civil rights expert john a. powell (2015) identifies belongingness as a manifestation of inclusion and shared humanity in the midst of diverse perspectives, identities, and ideas.

- **Microaggression:** Charles M. Pierce coined the term *microaggression* in 1978. He describes it as "subtle, stunning, often automatic, and nonverbal exchanges which are put downs by offenders" (Pierce, Carew, Pierce-Gonzalez, & Willis, 1978, p. 66). In 2010, Derald Wang Sue extended the definition of *microaggression* to include any marginalized group in society that become targets—people of color, women, LGBTQ+ persons, people with disabilities, religious minorities, and so on.

All biases discussed in this book are well researched and important to understand in the quest toward more equitable and inclusive education. Some of these biases have been researched since the 1940s and are now categorized into two types: *implicit* or *subconscious* and *explicit* or *conscious*. To date, not many books explore specific biases, the impact of biases on education, nor strategies to navigate through these biases. This book offers an understanding of biases beyond those that are implicit and explicit. As with most things, the more specific the knowledge, the better we can identify those biases that live in our conscious and subconscious minds. In addition to exploring specific biases that go beyond the common implicit and explicit biases, this book also provides implications for learning for all educators to recognize and manage our biases.

# Who This Book Is For

I wrote this book with every educator in mind, including myself, as counteracting biases is intentional and often daily work. This book is for every well-intentioned educator who genuinely wants to cultivate systemic equity, inclusion, and belongingness. Since Abraham Maslow first introduced the hierarchy of needs in 1943, we have known safety and belongingness are precursors to students' cognitive development. Creating more equitable and inclusive school communities is not a one-workshop or one-book job (Maslow, 1943). This work requires in-depth awareness of and strategies to counteract the biases that create the communities of exclusion we desire to change. For this reason, this book is for *all educators*. The scenarios in this book for each bias illustrate that biases are ingrained in every layer of education from K–12 to secondary, postsecondary, and beyond. Additionally, these scenarios are based on personal and lived experiences crafted with the intention of helping us see ourselves and the harm our unchecked biases cause.

*If you are a teacher*, after reading this book, you will be able to better identify your biases and utilize the tools presented to assist with counteracting behaviors rooted in bias that inadvertently cause some students to succeed while others do not. Further, you will become more acutely aware of specific biases impacting your relationships with students, with the focus of building a stronger sense of safety and belongingness in the classroom.

*If you are a district or building-level administrator*, you will benefit from this book because it explores specific strategies to support you as you develop unbiased policies that often directly impact equity, inclusion, and belonging. I encourage you to make trainings about specific biases discussed in this book mandatory. This can happen through face-to-face or virtual trainings that occur throughout the school year . . . not one and done!

Finally, *if you are an instructional coach or a professional development consultant*, you may utilize this book as a resource when supporting school communities to develop practices to ensure systemic equity. You may use some of the Pause and Ponder questions and activities as strategies to coach teachers and other educators in creating equitable classroom practices. Additionally, use this book as a foundation for professional development. Engaging in book talks that delve into each chapter will be of great benefit to your school community.

Navigating through personal and organizational biases supports schools in cultivating cultural proficiency and culturally relevant teaching and learning practices. Use this book as a resource on your journey to

> Navigating
> through
> personal and
> organizational
> biases supports
> schools in
> cultivating
> cultural
> proficiency
> and culturally
> relevant teaching
> and learning
> practices.

improving the culture of teaching and learning outcomes for everyone within and around your school community.

# What's in This Book

This book serves as a companion to other books focused on equity, culture, leadership, DEI, blind spots, inclusion, social justice, access, achievement gaps, and belongingness. Throughout this book, you will gain clarity on specific types of biases, how to recognize them, and tools for counteracting them. This book uses broad terms, such as *implicit (subconscious) bias* and *explicit (conscious) bias*, and develops concrete ideas about what these biases look like and how they show up in our practice as educators. Each chapter explores a specific type of bias that plagues school communities and leads to inequitable policies and practices.

Chapter 1 focuses on the importance of understanding specific biases and their connection to education. It examines how people's brains are hardwired to make decisions based on first thoughts because it is often the easiest route to decision making—but it is also often plagued by bias. Finally, it discusses the origin of biases and clarifies why even the most well-intentioned people can create inequitable environments because of bias.

Chapter 2 explores the Dunning-Kruger effect bias, which explains our resistance to being open to what we do not know. This type of bias often occurs in leadership positions and other positions of authority.

Chapter 3 focuses on herd mentality bias, which is deeply rooted in our desire to belong. Belongingness and connection are human needs. This chapter explores the various identifiers of herd mentality bias.

Chapter 4 focuses on anchoring bias. This cognitive bias impacts our decision-making processes because we focus just on what we know. It involves looking for information that validates or confirms our thoughts, as opposed to seeking and being open to information that may counter what we already know.

Chapter 5 discusses decision fatigue bias and the importance of timing when making important decisions that impact others. This bias may resonate with many educators, regardless of positionality or role.

Chapter 6 explores in-group bias, which relates to the way people make decisions based on familiarity and similarities. I examine implications regarding how this bias impacts the way we make decisions that affect those in both our in-groups and out-groups.

Chapter 7 focuses on scarcity bias and its ability to cause decision making rooted in the desire to avoid losing what we value most. Time, energy, and financial resources are precious commodities. This chapter sheds light on decisions we tend to make when we are afraid to lose something we value, particularly time, energy, and money.

Finally, the epilogue offers a synthesis of the biases discussed in the aforementioned chapters and inspires a call to action. It also provides hope and additional strategies for recognizing, as well as managing or counteracting, biases that pervade school communities.

Each chapter contains fictional, school-based scenarios involving administrators, teachers, counselors, professional development consultants, instructional coaches, and parents to illustrate that regardless of titles or positions, people's biases inadvertently derail their quest for equity, inclusion, and belongingness. This is done intentionally, as unfortunately, there is no sector of education immune to the damage unchecked biases can cause.

Although they are based on firsthand experiences, these scenarios are crafted with the intention of helping you see how specific biases left unchecked can cause harm to students, faculty, staff, parents, and all stakeholders in school communities. It is my hope that these scenarios spark intentional conversations and reflection to help counteract the biases that lead to inequitable communities in which some students are denied the universal need to belong. Throughout this book, I examine the root of specific learned biases and learning strategies to counteract biases so their negative impacts do not continue to permeate schools and further alienate the students we are here to serve.

# Conclusion

As educators, we have a moral and professional obligation to shape the intellectual and social abilities of our students. When we do not develop strategies to counteract our biases, they will surely show up in classrooms and throughout school communities, and the policies or equity plans that we develop will not be followed with fidelity because the root will be rotten. As we journey to recognize the specific biases that cause inequities in education, we will see a change.

The work of cultivating equity, inclusion, and belongingness in schools is a labor of love. I believe wholeheartedly in the redemptive power of people. I believe that with a growth mindset, effective strategies, and a commitment to apply those strategies, people and institutions can change, and students will receive a more equitable and inclusive education. Believing that people can develop their abilities and engage in a process to ignite change is the essence of a *growth mindset*, which Carol Dweck (2016) defines as the "belief that your basic qualities are things you can cultivate through your efforts, your strategies, and help from others" (p. 7). May the fruits of our labor be self-actualized in our schools and may generations of students benefit from the work we do to cultivate systemic educational equity, inclusion, and belongingness. Let us heal the roots.

> The work of cultivating equity, inclusion, and belongingness in schools is a labor of love.

CHAPTER 1

# Bias in Education

*If you don't know where you are going, any road will take you there.*

—Ugandan Proverb

Since 2006, I have facilitated professional development related to equity. During my work with supporting schools in closing equity gaps through disaggregating data, I have had the opportunity to work with educators in both K–12 and higher education, including superintendents, district-level administrators, instructional coaches, teachers, faculty, and others throughout various school communities. When I ask participants to write the definition of *equity* on an index card, I always receive multiple definitions, which often include keywords such as *equal*, *fair*, and *justice*. In a 2017 national study conducted by the Council of Chief State School Officers (CCSSO), dozens of educational leaders at the school, community, district, state, and national levels, who represent broad demographic and political diversity, were asked to define and describe *equity* and *inequity* in their own terms. There was no one answer at that time.

Unfortunately, there are various definitions of equity used in educational settings. Throughout this chapter, I explore the historical context of the term *equity*. It is important to note that while there are various definitions for equity, there is one thing for certain—*equity* and *equality* are not synonymous! They are not the same. As you read the next section and subsequent chapters, it is my hope you will have a clearer understanding of equity and its relationship to bias, as well as how certain biases impact our school communities.

# The Meaning of Equity

Merriam-Webster defines *equity* as "justice according to natural law or right; freedom from bias or favoritism" (Equity, n.d.). This definition clearly lends itself to the framework of this book, which is that biases create inequities. The National Equity Project (2024) defines *equity* as "each child receives what they need to develop to their academic and social potential." The National Equity Project (2024) explains that school equity also involves the following.

- Interrupting inequitable practices, examining biases, and creating inclusive multicultural school environments for adults and children

- Ensuring equally high outcomes for all participants in our educational system

- Removing the predictability of successes or failures which currently correlate with social or cultural factors

- Discovering and cultivating the unique gifts, talents, and interests that every human possesses

A good analogy to educational equity is the equity one might build in their home. In the book *Private Equity Accounting, Investor Reporting, and Beyond,* Mariya Stefanova (2015) explores the importance of home equity. Over time, the equity you build increases the value of your home. Equity can also be liquidated into cash should the need arise for emergencies, home improvements, or a dream vacation. The report *Making Use of Home Equity: The Potential of Housing Wealth to Enhance Retirement Security* highlights equity as a preferred way to accumulate assets in life (Ayuso, Bravo, & Holzmann, 2019). Therefore, equity in homeownership is a highly preferred way to accumulate assets. So, it is safe to say that equity is a good thing. It is valuable, it is important, and it is a commodity one can intentionally cultivate. Without it, homes could be lacking in value, which unfortunately, is the state of many schools and districts.

We measure equity in housing in assets and liabilities. In education, we must also begin to directly identify our assets and our liabilities, which go beyond race, ethnicity, sexual orientation, socioeconomic status, ability, gender, and more. However, sometimes educators consider students as liabilities instead of assets. For example, in a data team meeting at my school, teachers and administrators spent approximately forty-three minutes discussing one student whose parents were both in jail and how he would also "end up in jail someday." The purpose of this meeting was to analyze student data to discuss and plan for instructional strategies to maximize student achievement, so I calculated the amount of time they spent on this one student.

I thought it was interesting that, although we were able to disaggregate data to close the equity gaps in literacy and mathematics, the bulk of the meeting was spent talking about everything but academic data. Because this was a small community, many of the teachers and administrators were alumni of the school district and grew up with many of the students' parents. Outside of venting about the parents and student behaviors, no meaningful work was done to assist students academically during this meeting.

One of the effective means of cultivating equity in instruction is intentionally focusing on student data to make instructional decisions to meet their needs (Fisher, Frey, Almarode, Flories, & Nagel, 2019; Hollie & Muhammad, 2011; McKenzie & Skrla, 2011). Teachers did not walk out of the meeting with a clear picture of next steps in academic instruction for their students, which is both professionally unethical and counterintuitive to building equity in education.

As a teacher, I understand that there are times we need to vent; however, when venting supersedes intentionally looking at data to plan instruction for all students in the class, it becomes a source of inequity. In this case, the conversations about one student's behavior superseded planning instruction for the entire fifth-grade class for which they were supposed to be designing instruction for the upcoming week. Because there is a myth that inequity has more to do with race than any other factor, it is important to note that this was a predominantly White school in a rural district.

## Equity and Race

In 2015, the Every Student Succeeds Act (ESSA) was passed. For the first time in the history of the United States, the word *equity* became associated with education (U.S. Department of Education, 2015). The law stipulates that all schools must "advances equity by upholding critical protections for America's disadvantaged and high-need students" (U.S. Department of Education, 2015, p. 72.) Although there are many ways to advance equity in education, including ensuring equity in the distribution of highly qualified teachers, financial resources, academic supports, professional development, curriculum, culturally relevant teaching practices, and so on, it seems that equity became synonymous with race, as many authors and educational researcher focused on racial equity as a means to uphold ESSA (Collado, Hollie, Isiah, & Jackson, 2023; Neitzel & Mead, 2023; Perry, Zemelman, & Smith, 2022).

The reality is that racial equity is one of the many components required to achieve educational equity; however, there are other aspects that are important to advancing equity in education, as well. In my role as an equity trainer, I observed several teachers defining equity as equal treatment of students irrespective of race. Additionally, while assisting school administrators in creating their state-required equity plans, racial equity often became the topic of focus. Some school districts began to focus on racial inequity, while others continued their focus on equity as it related to recruiting and retaining effective teachers, improving classroom learning, and ensuring that teachers, administrators, coaches, mentors, and others within the school community had access to quality professional development. Interestingly, school districts that lacked racial diversity began to believe that they did not have any issues related to equity.

> Although race is a part of the equation on the journey to equity in education, it is not the sum total of this quest.

Again, it is important to understand that racial inequity is just one of the many types of inequities that plague schools. There are many evolving definitions and categories of equity in education, including, but not limited to, teacher preparedness, school leadership experience and mentorship, and guaranteed and viable curriculums that prepare students for postsecondary education and the workforce (Aguilar, 2020; McKenzie & Skrla, 2011; McNair, Bensimon, & Malcom-Piqueux, 2020; Hollie & Muhammad, 2011). Although race is a part of the equation on the journey to equity in education, it is not the sum total of this quest.

## Equity and Achievement for All

Too often, educators discuss equity through the lens of race, which can lead some predominantly White schools to believe that issues of equity are of no concern for their students and staff. Nothing could be farther from the truth. John Waters, director of the Regional Professional Development Center in St. Louis, Missouri, stated, "Wherever there is more than one student, there exists the possibility of inequity" (J. Waters, personal communication, December 12, 2018). Conversations and instructional plans must deliberately focus on student achievement for *all students*. When goals do not match our actions, we create unintentional inequities.

> **When goals do not match our actions, we create unintentional inequities.**

I don't believe that a well-intentioned educator wakes up and says, "Today, I am going to create inequities for my students." Educators often unintentionally create inequities because they are not deliberate enough about their educational practices, conversation, policies, and so on. Sometimes, we feel ashamed that we carry biases and have made instructional decisions that did not align with our values. Forgive yourself and remember the following quote from Sharroky Hollie (2012):

> The reality is our biases never completely go away. They simply recede or change, which is why it is important for you to know your biases, be in control of your thought processes, and be prepared to go responsive when necessary. (p. 31)

Just as a person purchasing a home must learn and be intentional about the community, home improvements, mortgage payments, and refinancing to build equity in their home, educators must become more intentional about cultivating equity in education to make that paradigm shift in education in which the assets (student achievement) outweigh the liabilities (students who do not achieve). Equity is a good thing!

> **Equity is a good thing!**

Urban and rural schools have similar issues when it comes to equity. For example, teachers in both rural and urban sectors of education often face issues with access to high-quality professional development opportunities. Continuous, high-quality professional development is a crucial factor in sharpening educators' skills to meet the needs of all students (DuFour, DuFour, Eaker, Many, Mattos, & Muhammad, 2024; Hollie & Muhammad, 2011).

In addition, both urban and rural schools struggle with obtaining substitute teachers to allow time for educators to participate in professional development opportunities, and they experience financial constraints to affording high-quality professional development. Regardless of race, students in lower socioeconomic communities often graduate from high school reading well below proficiency due to other inequities related to placement and availability of ineffective, out-of-field, and inexperienced teachers and administrators (Anderson, 2017; DiAngelo, 2018; Steele, 2011).

Issues related to inequity in education impact us all, especially for rural and urban students and their families. We must dig deeper and deliberately examine the inequities in schools, including, but not limited to, race. Casually discussing equity without recognizing and examining the biases that cause inequities and intentionally leveraging strategies to create systemic equity will not work. As the late James Baldwin stated in his 1962 *New York Times* essay, "As Much Truth as One Can Bear," "Not everything that is faced can be changed, but nothing can be changed until it's faced" (p. 38).

Therefore, to borrow a term from Angela Duckworth (2016), we must become "gritty" about the equity policies and practices that we cultivate in schools if we are to create more assets rather than liabilities in our education systems. Equity work requires grit "to keep putting one foot in front of the other . . . to invest, day after week after year, in challenging practices . . . to fall down seven times, and rise eight" (Duckworth, 2016, p. 275).

## Obstacles to Equity

Equity in education is possible. It is possible to educate a diverse population of students and equitably meet their educational needs. However, this does not come without obstacles or struggle. And when the obstacles come from within, it's important for the thought processes that created these inequities to change. Until they change, they cannot undo inequities. This could explain why schools that have developed equity plans still have considerable inequities. Healing inequity requires every educator to develop real clarity in understanding their own biases and implement strategies to counteract the effects of making biased decisions that create more inequity in schools. With millions and generations of students' lives at stake, we can no longer afford to create Band-Aid policies practiced without fidelity. Examining and creating solutions for the biases that lead to inequities is an imperative task that will lead to the systemic changes we need and desire for students.

There is no shortcut to achieving equity. Many districts focus on broad views of implicit and explicit bias, which, while necessary, are not specific enough to really move the needle on cultivating long-term equity in schools. To move the needle on equity, we must get specific about the types of biases that cause the inequities through which students are suffering in schools every day.

> We can no longer afford to create Band-Aid policies practiced without fidelity.

## The Difference Between Equity and Equality

In examining how we define equity, it is important to note that just as with the aforementioned study by the CCSSO (2017), there are various definitions for equity in education. This is a critical point, as equity is a term that is still fairly new in education, and we are "building the plane as we fly it."

*Equity* and *equality* are not the same, although many people use these terms interchangeably. As discussed in the introduction, *equity* involves ensuring every student receives what they need to develop to their academic and social potential (National Equity Project, 2024). *Equality*, on the other hand, is defined as being of the same quantity or importance (Equality, n.d.). For example, when students in the same grade and classroom receive the same assignments with no regard for those with individualized education plans (IEPs) or other accommodations based on their disability status, though this is *equal*, it is certainly not *equitable*. When students in the same grade and classroom receive assignments modified for those students with IEPs, this creates an equitable opportunity for all students to succeed.

Given the diversity of U.S. schools, the needs of one student often differ from another student's. It is our responsibility as professional educators to meet the needs of *all* students. Just as a medical doctor meets the diverse needs of their patients, a good educator intentionally assesses the needs of their students and uses intentional strategies to ensure all students succeed. I can tell you firsthand that this takes both internal and external work.

Internally, we must reflect on our practices while also managing our biases. Externally, we must create policies and practices that cultivate equitable learning experiences for all students. Ensuring all students have access to the same quality education does not negate the importance of an equitable education. For example, while coaching a third-grade teacher, I noticed one of the students struggling with the concept of butterfly metamorphosis. Some students were able to visit the local insectarium where there was a butterfly garden. The insectarium was quite expensive, which was a barrier for some families in this community. Through the lived experience of going to the insectarium, those who could afford to visit understood the process of metamorphosis much better than those who had not visited. Those students who had background knowledge about metamorphosis were visibly able access the learning material easier. This was evident in their quizzes as well. The students who visited the insectarium aced the quiz. The students who did not have the same lived experience did not pass the quiz. Granted, there could have been other factors that led to students not passing the quiz; however, one thing was clear—the students who could afford to go to the insectarium performed far better than the students who could not.

> Ensuring all students have access to the same quality education does not negate the importance of an equitable education.

One way the teacher could have made this an equitable learning opportunity was to give students a pre-test on metamorphosis. Additionally, bringing in butterflies, taking students on a field trip to the insectarium butterfly garden, or showing videos on metamorphosis to build background knowledge is another student engagement strategy that could have closed this equity gap. In this situation, all the students in the class were White, which proves that equity and the lack thereof is not always about race. Being in the same or equal learning environment is different than being in an equitable one.

# Equity in Schools

In 2013 and 2014, The National Center for Education Statistics showed that for the first time in U.S history, there were more Asian, African American, and Hispanic students in K–12 public schools than non-Hispanic Whites. The number of students of color, including Black and Indigenous students, in K–12 public schools had already reached a majority in 18 percent of the Western and Southern states during the 2011–2012 school year (National Center of Education Statistics, 2011, 2012). Simultaneously, the percentage of students with disabilities, as well as those from lower socioeconomic households, increased from 14 percent during the 2019–2020 school year to 15 percent during the 2022–2023 school year in K–12 public schools since the COVID-19 pandemic (National Center for Education Statistics, 2024). Given these statistics, it is safe to say that schools are growing increasingly diverse in various areas. Because education has the ability to change lives, it is imperative that educators are skillful at teaching students from diverse backgrounds and perspectives.

> Because education has the ability to change lives, it is imperative that educators are skillful at teaching students from diverse backgrounds and perspectives.

# Equity in History

In December 2015, the United States enacted the Every Student Succeeds Act (ESSA). This bipartisan law reauthorized the Elementary and Secondary Education Act (ESEA), originally signed in 1965, with the goal that every student would receive a "full educational opportunity" (DuFour, Reeves, & DuFour, 2018; Hess & Eden, 2021). As with the original law, ESSA is deemed a civil rights law, as for the first time in history, it became mandatory for schools across the United States to teach students to high academic standards to prepare them to succeed in college and careers. Civil rights are pillars of democracy that guarantee social opportunities and protection under the law irrespective of race, gender, religion, disabilities, and other characteristics (Dierenfield, 2007; Jeffries, 2019).

To support schools in ensuring educational equity, the U.S. Department of Education developed guidance and resource materials intended to support districts to address the inequities in their schools (U.S. Department of Education, 2015). These resources were shared as the White House held an inaugural convention attended by a team of principals, teachers, and superintendents from across the United States. The purpose of this convention was to advance the national conversation on positive school climates, which includes equity (U.S. Department of Education, 2015). With the support of the Department of Education, states were required to identify and address any inequities in resources for schools that needed support and improvement. School districts across the United States are now mandated to address inequity in schools specifically related to out-of-field, inexperienced, and ineffective teachers.

As an equity trainer, I noticed that some schools took their efforts a step further and began addressing inequities in all facets of education, including literacy, hiring practices, professional development opportunities, differentiating learning for gifted and struggling students, and so on. Within the ESSA plans submitted to the U.S. Department of Education, districts were required to outline how they planned to address equity concerns. As schools provided the same context of addressing specific types of inequities within their schools, this led to broader conversations about other inequities throughout various states, and school districts.

Because *equity* is still a new term in education, many states have different definitions. The state of Arizona defines *educational equity* as all students being provided with the resources they need to produce comparably positive academic and social outcomes regardless of race, ethnicity, gender, gender identity or expression, sexual orientation, language, religion, nationality, immigration status, cognitive or physical ability, family background or structure, income, or zip code (Arizona School Boards Association, n.d.). Arizona furthers its definition by providing insight into its guidelines for workplace equity, diversity, and inclusion in the Arizona Department of Education. This means that all staff, regardless of position, role, work experience, and work style are valued for their expertise, treated with respect, receive support to excel, and have equitable outcomes regarding the development and advancement of their careers.

The Illinois State Board of Education defines *equity* as having high expectations for every learner and providing supports and resources so each learner can meet those expectations (Illinois State Board of Education, 2022). The State of New York

Department of Education (2021) adds that students are to be in supportive environments where they are valued and respected irrespective of differences, including immigration status (New York State Education Department, n.d.). Although states do not have identical definitions for the term *equity*, healing inequity requires that educators work to heal, or at least consciously counteract, the biases that we bring to work with us.

I encourage you to look at the definition of *equity* in your state as well as the equity plan for your state and local school districts. As you review your state or organizational definition of equity, understand that it may be individual and collective biases that are impeding our understanding and our policies and practices that govern our schools.

In schools, *equity* is not a nebulous term, concept, or idea. It is a condition that can be measured and requires acknowledgment of biases that create inequity and a commitment to healing. Equity involves providing resources and support to students based on their needs, which means, as the professional adults hired to fulfill their academic needs, we need to identify their needs and get beyond the biases that prevent us from doing our jobs. Dwaun Warmack, former president of Harris-Stowe State University once said, "If you are not sitting at the table, then you are on the table" (D. Warmack, personal communication, August 22, 2017).

Often, when we make decisions without the insight of those for whom we are making decisions, we make mistakes. For example, if a school was planning an event celebrating Native American Heritage Month, including educators or students who are members of this demographic as part of the planning committee would be especially important. Without their insight, we risk offending the very demographic we seek to celebrate because they are "on" the table instead of "at" the table. Although we are professional educators, we do not know it all. Sometimes, we need to intentionally include other members of the school community to assist with planning events, especially in matters where we lack experience or expertise.

## Equity and School Culture

Diversity, equity, and inclusion are key aspects of improving school culture. Too often, the same people who created inequity in school districts and in classrooms are responsible for solving the inequity challenges in their districts. This can be difficult when there are no educational stakeholders at the table who have a different lens and background on improving equity. Therefore, issues related to equity in schools are prolonged because neither the right people nor the right mindsets are sitting at the table. Similar to the journey of culturally responsive teaching, which involves bringing students where they need to be academically by meeting them where they are both linguistically and culturally, the journey to equity requires both learning and managing our biases (Hollie, 2018). The journey to equity in schools also requires that we valiantly, consistently, and intentionally leverage our learning to check our biases. It is my hope that this book will aid in that process for years to come.

Many states, school districts, and universities have created positions designed to facilitate equity conversations and training. Sharing concrete data with school districts allows them to identify the inequities, and it is paramount for creating effective training designed to support them in developing equity plans and close equity gaps. As many districts submit their equity plans laced with policies to the department of education in their respective states, I wonder, "How can the same lens or policies that created inequity repair inequity?" Creating equity plans and policies are often not enough. When policies are not supported by practices, they become binders stacked in a district office or in the online district portal that are not truly practiced. We must take a deep look at behaviors and beliefs that have created and continue to create inequities in schools.

> Honoring the diversity of school communities while cultivating equitable and inclusive educational opportunities is a process.

In his webinar "Eazy-E: Oversimplifying Equity and the Harm It Causes," Howard E. Fields III (2021) emphasizes that there is no easy way out of inequity in education. Honoring the diversity of school communities while cultivating equitable and inclusive educational opportunities is a process. Just as making improvements to your home to beautify and increase its equity or value involves repairing the foundation or the pipes, the educational equity process can be a little rugged. True equity—systemic and long-term—requires repairing the foundation.

As the definition of equity continues to evolve, dig deep to recognize the roots of inequity more explicitly, beyond implicit and explicit bias, to create the systemic change in behavior so greatly needed. It is my goal to keep conversations about equity front and center, so it does not become a temporary buzzword in education, as equity is the heart of what I consider the new civil rights movement. While the Civil Rights Movement provided the foundation for desegregation and equal rights in politics, education, and other facets of the social and cultural fabric of the United States, disparaging data regarding educational attainment or academic achievement based on socioeconomic, racial or ethnic demographics, or gender and other characteristics imply that there are equity gaps that schools need to address (Borrero & Bird, 2009; Carter, 2010).

## Equity and the Future

The work of equity is the next layer of what civil rights leaders such as Medgar Evers, Paul Robeson, Barbara Jordan, Mary White Ovington, Richard and Mildred Loving, Jesse Jackson, Jack Greenberg, Septima Poinsette Clark, Rabbi Abraham Joshua Heschel, Martin Luther King, Jr., Coretta Scott King, Julius Rosenwald, Richard Morrisroe, Edith Stern, Angela Davis, Thurgood Marshall, Fannie Lou Haymer, Father Albert Foley, Jonathan Myrick Daniels, and countless others would want for education for future generations. In education, we must continue to work so that years from now, our children and our children's children are not suffering the from the ills of educational systems that do not intentionally value the diversity of race, gender identity, age, ability, thought, sexual orientation, religion, political affiliation, socioeconomic status, and so on.

The advent of social media gives us twenty-four-hour access to personal, institutional, global, and local news related to inequities in education and much more. Unfortunately, although equal rights are protected by law, our lives, liberty, and pursuit of happiness are being stifled due, in part, to educational inequity. As we intentionally recognize, examine, address, and leverage our learning of specific biases and strategies to counteract them, generations could be impacted by our efforts. Biases that become part of the subconscious thought process, as well as biases that we consciously choose because of our surroundings, are important for every educator to manage. However, to manage our biases, we must be able to identify them as well as employ strategies to navigate through them. Further analysis and understanding of the connection between the brain and biases will help further understanding on the root causes of biases.

# The Brain and Biases

The brain is an amazing organ. It holds both conscious and subconscious thoughts and stores information formulating one's values, ideas, and biases. As noted previously, Merriam-Webster defines *bias* as "(1) an inclination of temperament or outlook, *especially* a personal and sometimes unreasoned judgment; (2) an instance of such prejudice; or (3) a systematic error introduced into sampling or testing by selecting or encouraging one outcome or answer over another" (Bias, n.d.). Biases can be innate or learned. People may develop biases for or against an individual, a group, or a belief. In science and engineering, bias is a systematic error.

Subconscious thoughts are products of a person's upbringing and environment. Think about how many times you have seen billboards, magazines, and other advertisements that highlight only one body type, eye color, race, or gender. Think back to the family conversations you were part of or overheard as a child. Think about the movies, commercials, and television programs you grew up watching. All this information formed your views, values, judgments, and opinions about yourself and the world in which you live. The interactions you have as children and young adults, as well as the values you learn through your parents, religious affiliations, friends, community, television, social media, and other cultural conditioning, are crucial in forming emotional, cognitive, and behavioral biases.

> Biases are rooted in the subconscious, the part of the brain you are not fully aware of but influences your feelings, thoughts, and actions.

Unconsciously, people develop affinity for those with whom they are familiar and with whom they share similar views, values, cultural norms, religion, background, and other similarities (Steele, 2011). Thus, biases are rooted in the subconscious, the part of the brain you are not fully aware of but influences your feelings, thoughts, and actions (Fiske & Taylor, 2013).

According to Jean Piaget, a psychologist known for his theory of cognitive development, children understand the world through schemas—psychological structures that organize experience (Kail & Cavanaugh, 2019). As we get older, we begin to operate in the world based on the functional and conceptual knowledge that we learn. Understandably, unless we were raised or learned to question thoughts early in life, the brain becomes hardwired, thus creating prejudice (emotional bias), stereotyping (cognitive bias), and discrimination (behavioral bias), which may not be aligned with current views, values, goals, or best practices (Fiske, 1998).

## Mental Models

Psychologists have noted that from birth until the age of ten, people develop a formal understanding of the world in which they live, including values and views around society and the way they define themselves (Berk & Meyers, 2016; Coopersmith, 1974; Erikson, 1959/1994; Feldman, 2003). Unfortunately, as children, we have little to no control over the way parents, community, media, and social environment shape our mental models. Mental models become the catalyst through which we make decisions (Weinberg & McCann, 2019). In a perfect world, we would have mental models that align with our views and values. However, mental models can also be described as subconscious thoughts or views that are often contrary to our current views, values, and knowledge of best practices as educators.

I will use parent engagement as an example of the ways mental models can impact school communities. Many educators believe that parent engagement is important to students' overall social and academic growth. However, historically, there are issues bridging the gap between home and school. Often, schools don't ask parents to come into the school environment unless there are discipline issues, parent-teacher conferences, or the need for fundraising assistance.

While many schools do an amazing job intentionally creating schools as community hubs where parents, grandparents, and other community stakeholders are welcomed, there are still far too many schools that shun parent involvement. As educators, we can understand the importance of integrating parents and the school community, but we often miss the mark. Why is this? Could it be that subconsciously we do not want parents in the way of our pre-designed goals for students? Could it be that we do not trust parents and students' families to properly support them in the way that we see fit? Granted, building the bridge between home and school is a two-way street. Some parents neither want to get involved nor feel that they have the time; however, there are many parents who may want to be involved in their child's education but simply have not felt welcomed to do so.

It is important to recognize that sometimes our mental models or subconscious thoughts cultivate schools where parents do not feel welcome in the school community. We can change this dynamic. For example, one school in Chicago, Illinois, regularly invites parents to come sit with their children during the school day. They encourage them to come during the schoolwide independent reading time to sit with their children and read. The librarian also organizes dates throughout the week for parents to read aloud their favorite book with students. If parents do not have a favorite book, the librarian or teacher recommends books for them. The parent engagement at that school is excellent! This school often has a 98 percent participation rate during parent-teacher conferences and regularly hosts events such as chili cook-offs, movie Fridays, as well as other community events to intentionally strengthen the relationship between school and community.

On the other hand, there are schools in the same community that do not allow parents to visit classrooms during the school day out of concern that parents would cause a disruption. One of the schools that seemed to discourage parent involvement had a 43 percent participation rate for parent-teacher conferences and rarely hosted events that intentionally welcomed families into the school community. It is the role of the school board and the communities they serve to decide how to cultivate parent engagement. However, when you notice a difference between what a school says its values are and its actions that either encourage or discourage parent engagement, it is time to start asking what biases might be involved and how you might counteract them to build positive parent and school relationships.

Often, our biases and mental models are a result of our experiences. Some of those experiences are conscious, while some are based on unconscious experiences from childhood. The next section explores the slow and fast thinking that affect our judgments and decisions.

## Slow and Fast Thinking and Bias

The brain has two thinking systems: (1) slow thinking and (2) fast thinking (Gladwell, 2005). The fast-thinking system can make judgments almost immediately based on limited information. Malcolm Gladwell (2005) calls the process of making snap decisions "thin slicing." We use thin slicing when we act in prejudiced ways toward certain groups of people, as we allow our fast-thinking system to draw on flawed information and direct our actions without the slow thinking system. The slow thinking system is more deliberate, which we need when making decisions that do not come naturally or may require continuous effort (Kahneman, 2011).

Jennifer L. Eberhardt, a social psychologist at Stanford University, is noted for her work on bias, race, and inequality. In one of her TED Talks, Eberhardt (2020) states,

"Our brains determine how we act." If we want to change how we act, we must change our thoughts. Although everyone has implicit and unconscious biases, research shows that biases can be reduced through the very process of discussing and intentionally counteracting them with behaviors that mirror our true values (Banaji & Greenwald, 2013; Eberhardt, 2020; Kahneman, 2011).

> If we want to change how we act, we must change our thoughts.

Once we recognize our biases, we can reduce or manage them and control the likelihood that these biases will affect our behavior. For example, one can reduce unconscious negative bias toward a particular group through positive contact with members of that group and through "counter stereotyping," in which individuals are exposed to information that is opposite of the stereotypes they have about a group.

# Conclusion

As educators who have a moral and professional responsibility for molding the minds of students, it is our duty to examine and correct the thoughts that lead to the policies and practices in schools that create inequities and harm students' chances of competing in our global economy. It is imperative that we consciously identify and create strategies to counteract any biases that are counterintuitive to creating systemic equity.

If you have invested the time to read this introduction, thank you. Continue reading. I trust that this book will be a great resource for you and others in your educational network. As you read each scenario, think about various aspects of diversity, including, but not limited to, students with various races, ethnicities, genders, religions, disabilities, neurodivergences, sexual orientations, socioeconomic backgrounds, and so on. Although I was not able to include scenarios for all diverse categories in the world, I wrote this book with everyone in mind. Being a bias change agent begins now!

## CHAPTER 2

# Dunning-Kruger Effect Bias

*Ethics is knowing the difference between what you have a right to do and what is right to do.*

—Potter Stewart

Educators come to the field of education with various talents and skills, different levels of education, and myriad experiences that color their lens and shape the way they educate students. But sometimes, people, no matter their level of experience or education, inflate or overestimate their skills and abilities. This is called the Dunning-Kruger effect.

The Dunning-Kruger effect was named after psychologists David Dunning and Justin Kruger. In 1999, the Cornell University psychologists wrote a research paper titled "Unskilled and Unaware of It: How Difficulties in Recognizing One's Own Incompetence Lead to Inflated Self-Assessments" (Kruger & Dunning, 1999). In their research, they tested participants on grammar, logic, and sense of humor. They found that those who performed in the bottom quartile rated themselves far above average. Additionally, they discovered that people tend to overestimate their ability or knowledge in an area of which they have very limited experience. Kruger and Dunning (1999) write, "Often those with limited knowledge in a domain suffer a dual burden: not only do they reach mistaken conclusions and make regrettable errors, but their incompetence also robs them of the ability to realize it" (p. 1121).

Further, they indicate that being intelligent or knowledgeable in one area is not the same as learning or developing another skill.

Unfortunately, because many of us equate knowledge with self-confidence, we would rather pretend to be skilled in a particular area than appear ignorant or unknowing. Metacognition, or the ability to objectively think about one's thinking, is a key factor in the Dunning-Kruger effect, as they discovered that those who judged themselves to be above average did so because they lacked the ability to judge their own competence (Kruger & Dunning, 1999). Simply put, the Dunning-Kruger effect is a bias characterized by thinking we know more than we do and making decisions based on what we think we know.

> The Dunning-Kruger effect is a bias characterized by thinking we know more than we do and making decisions based on what we think we know.

When I first began working as a professional development consultant, the organization I worked with began discussing a new school that needed literacy training. Unlike the other schools we serviced, this was a predominantly Black school. We discussed the mentor texts we historically used to teach reading comprehension skills. Our job was to train and coach teachers on best practices of using mentor texts to deepen reading comprehension skills. Now that we were working with schools that were significantly more diverse, we decided to expand our mentor text selection we suggested teachers use in their instruction.

While we brainstormed other books to use as professional development tools, one of the seasoned trainers stated, "Kids are kids; we don't need different books to teach from. They will be fine with the text we use." She further stated, "All kids are the same, and they can read and learn from the same books." Then she asked, "Why do we have to change our practice just because these kids are Black?" As our director began to explain the research that supports the importance of diversity in mentor texts, the trainer pulled her chair away from the table, folded her arms, and said, "I don't need to hear any of this. I've been successful at working with teachers and kids for years without having to change a thing."

Although this literacy trainer was extremely knowledgeable in best practices in literacy instruction and coaching teachers, the inability to allow new learning to take root caused her to shut down. Although the information was there, she was not open to learning. When offered research that countered her belief, she was not open to expanding her toolbox of mentor texts to include diversity. Conversely, even when a school's demographics include only one race or one dominant race, it is important that students learn that we live in a remarkably diverse world. Learning about other cultures and ethnicities is a key factor in being successful in a global economy.

# All That I Know, I Know Not

The Yoruba people of West Africa coined the proverb, "All that I know, I know not," which is one of the guiding principles of Ifa, a spiritual philosophy or way of life that encourages good and gentle character (Karade, 1994). As educators, we know a lot, but it is important to humble ourselves and realize there is still a lot to learn.

Similarly, good educators are knowledgeable, creative, thoughtful, nurturing, and sometimes failing students. Even the best educator has students they are unable to fully reach. There's no harm in that. The harm is when we fail to stretch ourselves to be open to research-based best practices that provide us with new ways of thinking that will help reach students who we think are unreachable and close equity gaps we may think we are not able to close. Just as we can assume we "know it all," we can also approach each other and situations from a point of curiosity to seek new information. But it takes the mindset of a revolutionary change agent to study and apply new learning to significantly impact our classrooms and schools.

As educators, it is our moral and professional duty to do what is right for students. When I was a special education teacher in 2001, I remember when classrooms for students with neurodiverse, emotional, and physical disabilities were literally located in the basement. The decisions we make at the state, local, district, school, and classroom levels either advance students toward being adequately prepared for the global economy or not. Special education students who were placed in the basement as well as in general education classrooms were disadvantaged because they did not have the benefit of learning with and from each other. No one should be placed in the basement . . . literally or figuratively.

In part, the Hippocratic oath states, "I will not be ashamed to say, 'I know not,' nor will I fail to call on my colleagues when the skills of another are needed for a patient's recovery" (Hippocrates, ca. 400 B.C.E/1868). As educators, we are not bound by such a universal oath. However, to achieve equity in schools, it is important that we continually examine our actions. Through intentional reflection, we can ensure our actions align with best practices and what is right for students. Sometimes, this

> To achieve equity in schools, it is important that we continually examine our actions.

means being open to saying, "I don't know." We can bring information to educators, but we cannot make them open to applying new learning for the benefit of students.

# Bias Assessment

The checklist in figure 2.1 can help you assess your own Dunning-Kruger effect bias and check for the understanding of this specific cognitive bias. As you reflect on each descriptor, indicate the frequency in which you relate to each statement. Remember to be honest and give yourself grace. This is an opportunity to see yourself more clearly so you can respond in a way that prevents the negative impacts of the Dunning-Kruger effect bias in your school. Following the checklist are two scenarios that will assist in expanding your knowledge of how this bias shows up in schools.

| Descriptor | Most of the Time | Sometimes | Never |
|---|---|---|---|
| I ask for constructive feedback and criticism. | | | |
| I avoid constructive feedback. | | | |
| I consider and intentionally create a plan of action to improve and expand my knowledge based on the feedback or criticism I receive. | | | |
| I overestimate my knowledge or skills. | | | |
| I consider my successes and failures as elements that have added to the value of my life both personally and professionally. | | | |
| I acknowledge that within my profession, there are times when I am not the expert. | | | |
| I am comfortable seeking the assistance of others within and outside of my school community to assist in improving student outcomes. | | | |
| I overestimate my skill level. | | | |

| | | | |
|---|---|---|---|
| I often seek new knowledge and keep abreast of new research in my area of expertise. | | | |
| I recognize genuine skills in others, especially those who share similar roles and responsibilities in my school community. | | | |
| I recognize and acknowledge my own lack of knowledge of some aspects of my school community. | | | |
| I am modest and attentively listen to the ideas of others, especially when they are different from mine. | | | |
| I am aware of skills I don't have yet. | | | |
| I actively engage in professional development and other learning opportunities that expand my knowledge, even if I have experience and vast knowledge of the subject at hand. | | | |
| I am confident in my worth and abilities. | | | |
| The more I know, the more I realize how much more there is to know. | | | |

Reflect on your answers. Consider the following questions to guide your reflections.

1. In what situations have I overestimated my knowledge or skills?

2. How do I typically respond when I discover there is a gap in my knowledge or skills?

3. In what areas of my profession do I feel less knowledgeable or experienced, and how can I enhance my confidence and competence in these areas?

4. How do I typically handle situations in which I am not the expert?

5. Who within and outside of my school community can I approach for assistance or collaboration?

**FIGURE 2.1:** Dunning-Kruger effect bias self-reflection checklist.

*Visit **go.SolutionTree.com/diversityandequity** for a free reproducible version of this figure.*

Now that you have taken your personal inventory, read the following scenarios, which illustrate the impact of the Dunning-Kruger effect bias in schools. After reading each scenario, revisit the checklist to reevaluate your answers.

# Scenario 1

During an equity lab presentation for Calm School District, the superintendent, Mr. Jones, refused to participate. Equity labs were meetings with school administrators, teachers, and other educators that specifically focused on examining academic inequities or equity gaps within a grade level and throughout the school district. It was clear he had many years of experience and education, as he was able to cite research as well as observational data related to best practices in school improvement. He was polished, well-spoken, and well-educated. Unfortunately, Mr. Jones was superintendent of a school district that had several issues related to equity.

There were clear gaps in academic and behavioral data that indicated more liabilities than assets among several subgroups within the district. Data indicated that many students were performing above proficiency level, but there were no gifted programs nor supplementary activities available for high-performing students.

Longitudinal studies of these high-performing students indicated that those same students in one grade level showed a decrease in academic aptitude in the next grade level, which usually happens when there is no differentiation of instruction for high-performing students and more attention is given to students who are struggling academically.

High-performing students often assimilate to the culture of students who are receiving the most attention and support when their need for more rigorous instruction is not met. During the lab, the team navigated through presenting the data and areas of inequity the district needed to focus on, and all the participants, including the assistant superintendent and other district-level administrators, participated in the conversation, except for Mr. Jones. He believed the teachers and administrators were doing their best to support all students in their district. Although the data suggested otherwise, he did not budge from his stance that equitable education was being offered to all students.

Due to state-mandated reporting required to demonstrate efforts to address inequities in his district, he had to submit an equity plan focused on decreasing those inequities. As knowledgeable as the superintendent was about best practices in education and the demographics of the student body in his district, it was clear he did not know how to address the inequities.

Students who lived in neighboring communities, sometimes blocks away due to district boundaries, received different levels of education based on the school they attended. For example, there were two elementary schools within the district that were about five miles apart. Comparative analysis of third- through fifth-grade students attending these two schools showed that there were significant achievement gaps in the performance levels in English language arts (ELA). Students at school 1, which showed significant gains in ELA, were engaged in daily independent reading, guided reading, and whole-group instruction.

While facilitating other professional development for the elementary schools in the district, the team conducted instructional walks for the purpose of observing teachers utilizing effective teaching and learning practices based on John Hattie's (2023) research and collecting qualitative research to plan for the next steps in teacher training. The team observed several key differences in ELA instruction between school 1 and school 2.

1. The third- through fifth-grade classrooms in school 1 were print-rich, as defined by the U.S. Department of Education's *Implication for Practice in Early Childhood Programs* (Kadlic & Lesiak, 2003). Throughout the building, more noticeably in the fifth-grade classroom, there were story walls, updated bulletin boards, poems, charts, and examples of student work with effective feedback. Conversely, students in the same grade level at school 2 did not have the advantage of print-rich classrooms. Instead, there were very few instructional materials on the walls, and only outdated examples of student work were posted.

2. Students excelling academically in the third- through fifth-grade classrooms in school 1 consistently engaged in independent reading time that was embedded in their schedule every day. During independent reading, the team observed third-grade classroom teachers conferring with various students, engaging

them in intentional dialogue about what they were reading and focused on a comprehension strategy. However, students enrolled in some of the other third-grade classrooms in school 2 engaged in independent reading twice per week, with little to no engagement with their teacher. As educators, we know that students who engage in intentional, independent reading time throughout the week build stamina. Unfortunately, school 2's benchmark and yearly state testing showed that students struggled with reading stamina.

3. In school 1, students engaged in read alouds throughout the week during class in which teachers read grade level text and above in various third- and fifth-grade classrooms where students excelled academically. Their teacher asked thought-provoking questions as she read aloud, which stretched students' reading comprehension skills. Students who were reading below grade level had an opportunity to hear grade level vocabulary being used in the proper context. Additionally, these daily read alouds afforded students an opportunity to expand their knowledge of reading with expression. In school 2, read alouds did not occur at all.

The team shared these findings with the district administrators and were informed there were far more new teachers in school 2 compared to school 1, especially in ELA. Instead of allowing the team to steer the discussion toward research that would support those new teachers with professional development to teach the third- through fifth-grade students more adequately, Mr. Jones derailed the conversation by stating that his father used to be the superintendent of the very same district and that he grew up in that district. He began to share information about how he changed district leadership in an effort to increase diversity. Because this was a racially diverse school district, it was important to him that the administration mirrored the student population.

Mr. Jones was adamant about everyone in the district receiving diversity and inclusion training, which was commendable. However, it was clear that he did not want to entertain any further conversations about the academic inequities of these two elementary schools. After sharing information about the plan to recruit a new chief of diversity and inclusion, Mr. Jones said he was confident that this person was going to help steer the district in the right direction. He was under the impression that the equity issues in his district had more to do with race than with adequate teacher training, and the inequities specifically related to the level of academic rigor students were receiving in ELA.

Mr. Jones was gracious and thanked the team for coming to share equity data for his school district. To date, their district is celebrated for its stellar programs and events focused on diversity and inclusion. However, the gaps in the two elementary schools' ELA scores still exist.

# Scenario 2

Mrs. Cooper was a seasoned fifth-grade teacher at Dragonfly Elementary School. She had taught with the district for more than thirty years, and she was one of the most celebrated teachers in the building. As the demographics in the community began to change, Mrs. Cooper received more and more Hispanic and Latinx students. During an open-house event at the beginning of the school year where students and parents were scheduled to meet teachers for the first time, a parent noticed that all the posters and class materials included only White students. When the parents mentioned this concern, Mrs. Cooper stated that she prided herself on making sure all students received a quality education in her class. Up until recently, the demographics of her class only included White students. She mentioned some of the chapter books students read in her class included other races and ethnicities. However, among all the posters, educational materials, and library books in the classroom, none featured people of color.

Mrs. Cooper shared that she had many friends of other races and ethnicities. She felt defensive and told the parents that she resented any suggestion that she was not a good teacher. Although this is not what the parents said, it is what Mrs. Cooper heard. The parents spoke with the administrator about their concerns and were told that Mrs. Cooper was one of the best teachers in the building. Because of the value that this parent placed on cultural diversity and inclusion for her child, she asked that her child be placed in another classroom with a teacher who intentionally included other races and ethnicities in the classroom environment. Later in the school year, school administrators sent parents a climate and culture survey. The school district conducted a similar survey to assess the climate and culture for students. The results of the survey indicated the following.

- Students and parents in the non-White subgroups did not feel a sense of belongingness.

- Academic data, specifically mathematics and ELA, showed significant achievement gaps for students in various racial subgroups.

- Literacy rates for non-White students were significantly lower than those of their White counterparts.

- There were more suspensions and referrals for non-White students throughout each grade level in the building than for White students.

During an after-school meeting, the principal shared the school data with all the teachers. Mrs. Cooper, as well as others in the school district, began to attend professional development to improve their knowledge and awareness of strategies to improve DEI. Although she was not required to do so, Mrs. Cooper reached out to the parents who had raised concerns to apologize for being defensive. She told them she was investing in classroom materials that were more inclusive of the student body she served. She now understood it was important for all students to have materials in her classroom that represented, as well as celebrated, a diverse population of races and ethnicities. Mrs. Cooper's intentional efforts in this area of inclusion led her students to be among some of the top performing in the district.

---

In both scenarios, the superintendent and classroom teacher were knowledgeable and celebrated in their respective positions. In the first scenario, the superintendent reached the highest level of any administrator in the district. In the second scenario, Mrs. Cooper was one of the most celebrated teachers in her school. However, both educators exhibited what researchers call the Dunning-Kruger effect, as described earlier in this chapter.

# PAUSE AND PONDER

- How did the two educators in the scenarios demonstrate the cognitive bias known as the Dunning-Kruger effect bias?

- Recall a time when someone made a decision without considering all the necessary information. How did this decision impact you? How did you feel knowing they made this decision without all the necessary information? Were you angry, sad, hurt, or unsettled?

- Now, let's focus on students. Remember a time when you made a decision that impacted students without having all the necessary information, knowledge, or research. How did you know you didn't have all the information and that it was impacting students in a negative way? How do you think it made the students feel?

Since both Mr. Jones and Mrs. Cooper had great success and were highly celebrated in their respective positions, they had confidence in their leadership and abilities to foster student achievement. They were knowledgeable in one area; however, their *knowingness* and sense of confidence prevented them from recognizing, learning, and applying solutions that would drastically impact student achievement. This bias can be damaging to the learning environment because it leads to closed-mindedness. Mr. Jones focused so much on changes the district was making around diversity and inclusion that he derailed a conversation in which he could have learned more about the inequities causing the huge gaps in the ELA scores of the two elementary schools in his district.

Mrs. Cooper was so focused on the things she was doing well she did not consciously recognize that there were students who were not doing well, in part because they did not feel a sense of belongingness. A sense of belongingness is a basic need that involves feeling loved and accepted. It also includes the need to feel that one belongs to a social group, which encourages their ability to learn (Maslow, 1943). When students do not feel a sense of belongingness, they often shut down and do not perform as well as the dominant subgroup, which creates inequity.

Some may suggest that it is the student's responsibility to feel good about themselves, and it's the parent's responsibility to instill a sense of cultural pride in their children. However, when students are in school for more than 60 percent of their day, we must be mindful about the messages we send about who is worthy and who is not. In Mrs. Cooper's case, she learned that representation matters when creating an environment of learning that is inclusive and beneficial for all students.

Both Mrs. Cooper and the superintendent inadvertently developed the bias known as the Dunning-Kruger effect. Both educators prided themselves on their knowledge and expertise regarding the students they served. However, both Mr. Jones and Mrs. Cooper would have benefited from improving their openness and metacognition skills, which would require them to think about their thinking. When we practice metacognition, we are better able to ask ourselves if our actions align with our students' views and values. When we are led to water and are open to taking a drink, we begin to step outside of ourselves to ask or receive help. Thankfully, Mrs. Cooper was able to step outside her comfort zone and embrace practices of inclusion in her classroom.

## PAUSE AND PONDER

- As you reflect on each scenario and think about your own situation, ask yourself what information you wish someone considered when making a decision that impacted you. How would it have made you feel to know that the decision maker considered all the information before making that decision? Would you have felt grateful they considered all perspectives? Would you have felt valued, appreciated, and seen?

- Now, examine the situation you recalled earlier, in which you made a decision that impacted students. What information do you think would have been valuable to support you in making a more equitable decision? Why weren't you open to new information? How do you think students would have felt knowing you considered and asked for all pertinent information before making a decision that impacted them? Do you think they would have felt a sense of belonging or felt seen, valued, heard, and appreciated?

As a result of further training on equity, Mrs. Cooper realized she made decisions about her classroom based on subconscious thoughts and biases. She made an additional effort to address her behavior with the parents who had questioned her about her classroom practices. She applied her desire to educate all children equitably and began attending professional development to expand her learning.

Mr. Jones, along with the district administrators, submitted an equity plan to make sure they were compliant with the state's regulations. Regrettably, their equity plan focused on the diversity and inclusion initiatives in their district. School report card data from that district still shows a huge gap between students attending both elementary schools. If Mr. Jones "drank the water," or opened himself to engage in conversations about the inequities in ELA, amazing things could have happened for students and staff.

Furthermore, "drinking the water" would have led to Mr. Jones, as well as other administrators, to examine the types of support their elementary teachers were receiving. By addressing the inequities in ELA, they could have developed an action plan for enhancing professional development offerings that directly addressed the inequities in collective teacher efficacy and academic achievement.

## PAUSE AND PONDER

- Think back to a time in which you experienced a decision being made without all the necessary information. Why do you think the decision makers did not consider or ask for all the necessary information? Do you think they thought they knew all the necessary information? Can you presume positive intent, or do you think the decision was made blatantly without considering all the information? What could the decision makers have done differently? How did it feel?

- Remember a time when you made a decision students deemed unjust or premature because you did not consider all the information. Why do you think you did not consider all the information? How do you think your decision made students or colleagues feel?

In both scenarios, leveraging new learning is important to providing equitable solutions for students. We tell students all the time that education is a lifelong process. The same holds true for educators and leaders. As Mrs. Cooper began to learn more about diversity, equity, and inclusion through professional development, she realized that the same lens that created equity could not heal inequity unless that lens was changed. She applied her learning by diversifying her classroom library and posting learning materials and posters that celebrated a variety of races and ethnicities—this takes courage. (I discuss scarcity bias in more detail in chapter 6, page 103.)

Even if Mrs. Cooper's school continued as a predominantly White school, it is not in the students' best interest to only see people who look like them. This can be damaging and lead to a very narrow-minded way of thinking about the world. Additionally, as those students go off to college and careers, they will have to interact with people of other races and ethnicities. The best training ground for preparing students for a global society is both at home and at school. Even when a school's population is a majority of one race, it is in the students' best interest to see and learn about other races and ethnicities on a regular basis.

> Even when a school's population is a majority of one race, it is in the students' best interest to see and learn about other races and ethnicities on a regular basis.

Sometimes, schools that are predominantly White, or predominately Black, or predominant Hispanic or Latinx lean into only celebrating people of their same race or nationality. Not only is this damaging to students, but it also does not represent the real world in which they will eventually live. Mrs. Cooper counteracted the Dunning-Kruger effect bias by going outside her own thinking and knowledge base. She expanded her awareness and utilized what she learned to make the changes necessary so all students could achieve both academically and socially in her classroom. She began to understand what she had heard recently at a conference on equity—irrespective of race or ethnicity, if there are just two students, opportunities for inequities still exist.

Whether your student body is large or small or from one ethnic background or many, the possibility of inequities always exists. Therefore, it is important to continue learning. Continue cultivating your intelligence and stretching yourself to learn more about the students you serve and how to equitably support them in acquiring the academic as well as social skills necessary to excel in the global economy.

## PAUSE AND PONDER

- Think about the scenarios you discussed previously, when you, someone you know, or a student was impacted by a decision that was made without all the information needed.

- What tips can you leverage to help make a different decision in the future? Which specific strategy or strategies could you have used, and how could things have been different? What impact on the relationship with your students or colleagues do you think this different decision would make? How do you think they would feel? How would you feel?

As you complete your reflections, the goal is for you to revisit any institutional or classroom policies and practices that mirror the Dunning-Kruger effect. Moreover, the goal for us, as educators, is to acknowledge there are moments when, while we are proud of what we know, there is a plethora of information we do not know that can make us even better. We may see the Dunning-Kruger effect bias show up in our personal and professional lives. Ask yourself, "Am I open to new information? Am I allowing myself to expand and become better by learning and applying new information? In what areas of my life can I afford to stretch and learn more?"

Biases like the Dunning-Kruger effect do not just show up in our profession; we become masters of this bias by unconsciously practicing it day after day. There's much we know and can share with students and fellow educators; there is still much we can learn. You can learn to counteract this bias by simply reminding yourself that all that you know, you know not.

# Tips for Counteracting Dunning-Kruger Effect Bias

Paul Ziegler, CEO of a nonprofit educational service dedicated to providing leadership and resources to support learning, equity, and innovation to maximize student success, wanted to expand professional development opportunities for school districts (Education Plus, n.d.). So, he scheduled a meeting with every consultant throughout the company to get to know their background and expertise. He asked each consultant about their skills, interests, and ideas regarding professional development offerings for schools.

It was not enough for him to look at each person's resume and assign professional development topics based on each consultant's background. Leveraging the fact that each consultant may have an interest in expanding the professional development offerings and including them in that process afforded the organization great success.

Zeigler recognized there were things he did not fully know and understand about consultants under his tutelage. Proactively learning about the background of consultants and taking their professional development ideas into consideration yielded even more success for the organization. Consultants felt valued and purposeful in their work, which is the true measure of equity and inclusion.

While it is OK to not know everything, acting as if you do can be harmful, especially when you have a responsibility to make educational decisions that impact students' future success. Counteracting the Dunning-Kruger effect bias involves being proactive in seeking opportunities to fill any knowledge deficits you may have. This takes a great deal of courage and humility. When you allow yourself to expand your knowledge beyond what you think you already know, you are better able to cultivate equity and inclusion in school communities. In other words, "Drink the water!"

Following are some suggestions for counteracting Dunning-Kruger effect bias.

> When you allow yourself to expand your knowledge beyond what you think you already know, you are better able to cultivate equity and inclusion in school communities.

- Take a deep breath and ask yourself, "What information do I need to make the best decision for the students I serve?"

- Give yourself credit or a proverbial "pat on the back" for what you know, and then mentally remind yourself that learning is a lifetime process.

- Remember that expanding your knowledge sets a good example for students.

- Look at data on the decision you need to make and research best practices. If the research does not align with what you already know, use the new knowledge to expand your awareness and make the best decision for students.

- Listen to students and colleagues, regardless of their status. Remember that we can learn a lot from each other.

- Continue to attend webinars, conferences, and other forms of professional development so you stay abreast of any new research and strategies that enhance student achievement.

- Keep in mind that just because you don't know something doesn't mean that you aren't enough. Sometimes we place value on the amount of information we know and think not knowing depreciates our intelligence and value. Do not worry about not seeming like the smartest person in the room; consciously shift your concern by collecting information to make the best decision for the students you serve.

- Consciously remind yourself to stay open to new or contradicting information. Write this on a sticky note or say it in the mirror daily, "All that I know, I know not . . . *teach me.*"

- Join and stay engaged with a professional learning community specifically geared toward your role or goal as an educator.

# Next Steps

Chapters 2–7 offer an observation and assessment tool for you to reflect on each of the biases discussed. Figure 2.2 (page 52) shows a completed sample of the tool, using this chapter's topic as an example. The "Dunning-Kruger Effect Bias Observation and Assessment Tool" reproducible (page 53) can help you observe and

**Your Role:** Teacher

**Type of Bias:** Dunning-Kruger Effect Bias

**Description of Dunning-Kruger Effect Bias:** A bias characterized by having excessively favorable views of one's abilities in social and intellectual domains; acting as if you know more than you do.

| Questions | Answers |
|---|---|
| What do you observe in the classroom or larger school community related to this bias? | Our school principal makes decisions that impact us (teachers) without speaking with us. Recently, he made changes to our planning time schedule. We used to use this time to plan lessons together as a grade level. |
| What are some possible impacts on students? | Since some of the teachers in our grade level are new, it was helpful to meet to plan lessons together. Now students won't benefit from our planning time together. |
| What are some possible solutions? | Discuss the changes with our principal and ask that the grade-level planning time be reinstituted. |
| What are the next steps for accomplishing the solution? | Ask some of the other teachers in my grade level about meeting with our principal together. |
| What resources or assistance might be needed? | We need a different schedule that allows us collaborative planning time. We also may need to schedule some time together as a grade level to meet with the school principal. It might also be helpful to see if other grade-level teachers have the same concern and would like to with the school principal together. |

**FIGURE 2.2:** Sample completed Dunning-Kruger effect bias observation and assessment tool.

assess the incidences of Dunning-Kruger effect bias happening in the classroom or larger school community and plan next steps. You can use this tool regardless of your role in the school (teacher, administrator, coach, and so on). You can also share this tool with others in the community to obtain their feedback and suggestions.

# Dunning-Kruger Effect Bias Observation and Assessment Tool

**Your Role:** _____

**Type of Bias:** Dunning-Kruger Effect Bias

**Description of Dunning-Kruger Effect Bias:** A bias characterized by having excessively favorable views of one's abilities in social and intellectual domains; acting as if you know more than you do.

| Questions | Answers |
|---|---|
| What do you observe in the classroom or larger school community related to this bias? | |
| What are some possible impacts on students? | |
| What are some possible solutions? | |
| What are the next steps for accomplishing the solution? | |
| What resources or assistance might be needed? | |

## CHAPTER 3

# Herd Mentality Bias

*If you think you are too small to make a difference, you haven't spent a night with a mosquito.*

—African Proverb

Many of us have witnessed herd mentality or herd behavior on the local news. Riots and other types of protests are hallmark characteristics of herd mentality. Although we have watched this bias play out on television, it is much different when it impacts decisions affecting students or employees. As a literacy specialist, I had the pleasure of working with schools across the United States. One of the questions I would often ask is, "What's on your library shelves?" I invite you to do the same. Are certain ethnicities missing from the literature? Do the books on your shelves reflect your school's population and those of other communities, nations, and world? Are the books representative of what students in your school community like to do? If you notice that the books in your classroom or school libraries lack racial and ethnic representation, you may benefit from learning more about herd mentality bias.

## Crowd Characteristics

In the mid-1800s, French psychologist Gustave Le Bon coined the term *herd mentality* marking this type of bias as one of the oldest research-based biases. Le Bon (1895) used the term *herd mentality* to describe a person's unconscious tendency to follow others based on a shared ideology, belief, or idea. In his book *The Crowd: The Study of the Popular Mind*, Le Bon (1895) further described herd mentality as the "the turning in a fixed direction of the ideas and sentiments of individuals composing such a crowd, and the disappearance of their personality" (p. 9). Le Bon goes further, grouping the general characteristics of crowds into four categories.

1. The impulsiveness, mobility, and irritability of crowds characterized their ability to be "guided almost exclusively by unconscious motives" (Le Bon, 1895, p. 10).

2. The suggestibility and credulity of crowds, which refers to the "rapid turning of the sentiments of a crowd in a definite direction" (Le Bon, 1895, p. 14). It is an idea that turns into an act others often naively follow.

3. The exaggeration and ingenuousness of the sentiments of crowds. This describes them as individuals who gather and are moved by a feeling often stimulated by exaggeration that is "easily led into the worst excesses" (Le Bon, 1895, p. 22). He also notes that crowds can be "skillfully influenced . . . capable of heroism and devotion" even more than individuals acting alone to influence change (Le Bon, 1895, p. 22).

4. The intolerance, dictatorialness, and conservatism of crowds describe the tendency of them to follow "simple and extreme sentiments; the opinions, ideas, and beliefs suggested to them are accepted or rejected as a whole, and considered as absolute truths" (Le Bon, 1895, p. 24).

These four characteristics of crowds, as detailed by Le Bon (1895), can be observed in the media as well as in schools. Since actions and inactions are often ruled by ideas, I suggest it is also ideas about going along with the crowd that cultivate institutional policies and practices.

## Herd Mentality and Group Think

Seventy-three years after Le Bon researched and coined the term *herd mentality*, Wilfred Trotter, a British surgeon, popularized the term *herd behavior*. In his book *Instincts of the Herd in Peace and War*, Trotter (1916) describes how herd behavior and "group think" can negatively impact society and everyday decisions. Maybe for you, group think, or herd behavior, occurs in conversations at work; maybe it occurs during discussions about voting or political affiliations. Perhaps group think occurs when educators are deciding to support a particular initiative or policy that impacts schools. At times, it may be a fellow teacher, an administrator, or a board member who goes along with a particular decision they know would not be good for all students but votes in favor of it anyway because they don't want to be seen as difficult or fear being isolated from their peers. While this is understandable, when biases are left unchecked, more inequities in school communities might be created.

> When biases are left unchecked, more inequities in school communities might be created.

## An Example of Group Think

Early in my teaching career, I spent most of my lunch periods in the lead teacher's room to eat with the other middle school teachers. One day, we were discussing the influx of Colombian students enrolling in the school. Many Spanish-speaking students were coming into classes where none of us understood the language.

While we were fortunate to have some amazing English as a second language (ESL) teachers and translators, many of the middle school teachers who gathered during lunch complained about the stress of having Spanish-speaking students in their class. One teacher commented, "I don't think they should have the option of not speaking English when they are in our country." She went on to vent her frustration about having the option to press 1 for English and 2 for Spanish when she calls any customer service number.

As she shared her thoughts, other teachers chimed in to express their frustration about who they called "foreigners" taking over our country and our schools. I was speechless. As I listened to them, I lost my appetite, but I didn't say anything. Because of my history of being a middle schooler who attended a predominantly White school, I knew all too well how it felt to be an outsider. I remember being teased and not having anyone else to eat lunch with. That experience caused me to be consciously aware of the way I treat people who are different from the status quo, especially in a classroom setting. Still, I sat there listening to more than a handful of teachers go on about their disdain for people who don't speak English in America out of what I consider to be a false sense of patriotism.

Later in my career, I learned their comments were a form of xenophobia or prejudice against people from other countries (Makari, 2021). Looking back, I wish I had shared what I was thinking. By sharing my experience, I might have stimulated another thread of thought about inclusion. Maybe the other two teachers who were quiet during the conversation thought the same thing I did but didn't know what to say. Or, like me at the time, perhaps they did not want to say anything that went against the expressed thoughts of the lead teachers and others because they simply wanted to fit in. Although there was one teacher who didn't say anything, she would shake her head and eventually stopped having lunch with the other teachers.

I had a good relationship with our school principal, so I privately shared some of my concerns. I was concerned about how students would feel and be treated in a classroom where there was clear *anchoring bias*, which is discussed in chapter 4 (page 71). *Anchoring bias* is a cognitive bias in which "an individual's decisions are influenced by a particular reference point or 'anchor,' which is usually the first information they receive" (Tversky & Kahneman, 1974, p. 1124). But then I went to work in my own classroom, which had four new students from Colombia. Students adjusted to them being there; we learned new words and phrases that enriched our classroom learning experience; and the Colombian students began to learn English, which helped them to navigate more efficiently in their new country.

While this situation ended up as a win-win for students at that moment in that school year, I was still concerned about how their Spanish-speaking peers were being treated in other classrooms, especially with the teachers who passionately expressed their disdain for the Spanish-speaking community.

# Bias Assessment

Use the checklist in figure 3.1 to assess your own herd mentality bias and check for understanding of this specific cognitive bias. As you reflect on each descriptor, indicate how frequently you relate to each statement. Remember to be honest and give yourself grace. This is an opportunity to see yourself more clearly so you can respond in a way that prevents the negative impacts of herd mentality bias in your school. Following the checklist are two scenarios that will assist in expanding your knowledge of how this bias shows up in schools.

| Descriptor | Most of the Time | Sometimes | Never |
|---|---|---|---|
| I am comfortable sharing a different or opposing view from those of my colleagues. | | | |
| I am a leader among colleagues and often make decisions that align with them. | | | |
| In public settings, I gravitate to the front of the crowd. | | | |
| In public settings, I gravitate to the back of the crowd. | | | |
| I consider myself a risk taker and am open to new ideas. | | | |
| I am more comfortable sharing my ideas when in agreement with others. | | | |
| I am comfortable sharing my ideas even when no one in the room agrees with me. | | | |
| I tend to gather all the facts before making decisions, including listening to other perspectives. | | | |
| I tend to make decisions based on what I feel is best. | | | |
| I am comfortable speaking up and advocating for others. | | | |
| I worry about being ostracized if I speak up in opposition of popular ideas or opinions. | | | |
| I am confident in my ideas and opinions. | | | |
| I am the first to speak out about ideas and policies I believe to be harmful to others. | | | |
| I share ideas and offer suggestions for new school policies that may be helpful to others. | | | |
| I am comfortable being myself in a crowd. | | | |

Reflect on your answers. Consider the following questions to guide your reflections.

1. Do I feel more comfortable sharing ideas that align with others' opinions? If so, why?

2. What experiences contribute to my being uncomfortable sharing dissenting ideas?

3. What experiences have helped me become comfortable with sharing dissenting ideas?

4. What can I do to build confidence in sharing ideas that may not align with the majority?

5. What processes do I follow to gather facts and consider different perspectives before making decisions?

**FIGURE 3.1:** Herd mentality bias self-reflection checklist.

*Visit **go.SolutionTree.com/diversityandequity** for a free reproducible version of this figure.*

Now that you have taken your personal inventory, read the following scenarios, which illustrate the impact of the herd mentality bias in schools. After reading each scenario, revisit the checklist to reevaluate your answers.

## Scenario 1

Dr. Hayes was a seasoned educator who worked at the Journey School Consulting Agency. Before beginning her work with an agency that provided consulting and professional development for schools, she was a classroom teacher and administrator for thirty-five years. After she retired, she wanted to continue learning and sharing her experiences with other teachers. She began working for this consulting agency as a means of continuing her work as a lifelong educator. During her first meeting with the consulting agency, the director, along with the other consultants, met to give Dr. Hayes a brief overview of the schools they worked with and shared training materials.

As the directors and other consultants went down the list of schools they worked with, they stopped at one school and started singing "Welcome to the Jungle." Interestingly, the school that they were referring to was one with which Dr. Hayes was very familiar. It was a predominantly Black school located in an urban area that, in truth, had a lot of discipline concerns. However, there were other schools on the list that also shared similar discipline concerns. The key difference was that those other schools were predominantly White in rural areas.

As she watched and listened, Dr. Hayes noticed that there were twelve consultants in the room. Over half of them joined in to sing while others laughed. There were three others who put their heads down and smirked, seemingly uncomfortable with the interaction. Dr. Hayes was very uncomfortable as well, but since this was her first meeting, she did not feel comfortable rocking the boat and decided not to say anything. She kept quiet, but as they continued to sing every time they mentioned the school's name, she grew more and more irritated.

As the first African American woman to work for this agency, she was afraid that if she said something, they would deem her as an angry Black woman. She was also afraid that if she said something, she would be ostracized by the rest of the consultants. Being part of the team was very important to her, not only because these were her new colleagues but also because she prided herself on having good professional relationships with colleagues. Additionally, there was an understanding that the director assigned each consultant school based on experience. Staying quiet was also a protective mechanism for Dr. Hayes, as she wanted to ensure that she would get chosen to work with a school. Speaking up was very risky for her, but not doing so made her uncomfortable.

After two hours of hearing the song at least two more times when referring to that school, there was finally a break. Dr. Hayes went outside and called one of her trusted mentors who was the superintendent for another school district. She could trust that he would keep their conversations confidential, so she shared with him what was going on. She also shared that she was afraid of speaking out for fear of being labeled "the angry Black woman." He assured her that there was nothing angry about her, but she did have an obligation to speak up. He encouraged her to "ask the question." Asking the question is a way of assuming positive intent. It can neutralize the feeling of being accused, which can cause others to become defensive. They spoke on the phone for about ten minutes during the break, and then she went in with the confidence to "ask the question."

As soon as everyone came back from the break, Dr. Hayes gently shared her observation and then asked, "Do you all have theme songs for all schools we work with?" She explained that she observed earlier that every time they mentioned one school, they sang "Welcome to the Jungle." However, there were no theme songs for other schools they mentioned.

Interestingly, one of the senior consultants shared that the reason they sang that song is because every time one of them went into the school building, it was loud, and it didn't seem like the students really cared about education. Dr. Hayes was familiar with some of the other schools the consultant agency served. They, too, were schools that had discipline issues with students and high teacher turnover. This led Dr. Hayes to conclude that they sang "Welcome to the Jungle" to mock the predominantly Black school by comparing the school to a jungle. The director's next comment solidified her concern. She said that some of the consultants were afraid to go into that school and that was one of the reasons Dr. Hayes was hired. The director said she was hoping Dr. Hayes's experience with urban schools would make a difference.

Dr. Hayes asked the question because she knew about the discipline issues in that school and in at least three other schools they were working with, one of which had an issue with a student bringing a gun to school. This predominantly White school also had just installed metal detectors and had very similar academic concerns as the predominantly Black school. With that information, Dr. Hayes brought to their attention the discipline concerns with some of the other schools and decided to directly point out that her concern was one school was Black and the other school was predominantly White. She also explained that as someone new to the agency, she wanted to understand how schools were categorized and was concerned about the way in which this predominantly Black school was being characterized. She wondered how they could equitably serve a school that they refer to as "the jungle."

One of the consultants explained that she grew up in a rural area where her best friend was Black and resented the implication that they were singing this song to racially profile the school. Another consultant commented that some of their children's closest friends are Black, so they could not possibly be prejudiced. Keep in mind, Dr. Hayes had not used the terms racial profiling or prejudice when she asked the question.

Fortunately, one of the three consultants who had been quiet explained that the song reference made her uncomfortable as well, and she did not think they were doing a good job servicing the school because of their preconceived notions of the students. Another consultant went on to say that she was afraid to go to the school at first because of what they shared with her, but after going a few times, she realized that the school was no different from some of the other schools they serviced.

This comment seemed to spark a lot of other conversations, which led to the director apologizing for the jungle reference and asking that consultants not sing that song again when talking about that school. She said that they all have a lot to learn, and she was glad Dr. Hayes pointed out the concern. The director also said she was looking into some diversity awareness training for the agency because they included more ethnically diverse schools and wanted to ensure they were all properly trained to recognize their own biases.

She further pointed out that the success of the consulting agency would depend on all the consultants learning how to respectfully work with districts regardless of their ethnic and cultural backgrounds. Not only did she assign Dr. Hayes the predominantly Black school district, but she also assigned her three other schools. Dr. Hayes and one of the other consultants who spoke out worked together for several years. They helped improve the academic and discipline concerns with all the schools to which they were assigned with great success.

# Scenario 2

Amy was a new teacher with the Alona School District. She was excited to work in this district, especially since she grew up in the area and attended the elementary school where she was now on staff as a third-grade teacher. Every other week, each grade level engaged in data team meetings designed to look at student assignments and test scores with the purpose of supporting each other and developing next steps for students who were performing below, on, and above grade level. Each teacher was responsible for bringing samples of student work and often utilized the same assessments so they could have comparative data for all students on the same grade level. Some of the teachers she worked with in her grade level had been with the school district for more than twenty years.

Amy enjoyed working with her third-grade team because not only did she learn a lot from them, but they also seemed very intentional about including her in conversations and often asked for her suggestions. Like many school districts, all the teachers in her grade level were women; however, the principal was a man. After a few months of attending data team meetings, Amy noticed that every time the school principal attended the meetings, teachers stopped offering suggestions. Teachers in her grade level continued sharing data associated with each student and how they performed on weekly assessments, but whenever the male principal came to the meeting, they deferred all suggestions to him.

The first time Amy noticed it, she and the other teachers had been in the meeting for about forty-five minutes. During that time, they created solutions and made suggestions for activities to provide differentiated learning for students on various levels. When the principal walked in, he said, "Hey girls, where are we?"

Amy was not accustomed to being referred to as a "girl," but she followed her team's lead and did not say anything. The lead teacher and others brought him up to speed by sharing some of the assignments and problems they were experiencing academically with students. However, they did not share any of the collective suggestions or activities discussed when he was not there.

Instead of sharing their suggestions, the teachers asked him, "What do you think we should do?" Amy was confused and thought, "What just happened?" She started sharing some of the solutions and activities they discussed before the principal entered the room, one of the senior teachers tapped her hand and said, "That's OK; not right now." Amy was confused about what was going on and decided to just observe.

After a few months, Amy decided to ask her team why they decided not to share their suggestions and activities with the principal. She wanted to understand how they could be so brilliant to come up with all these assignments, suggestions, and activities to differentiate learning when he was not there but then turned to him for all the solutions when he was. This was a fair question that did not go over well with her fellow third-grade team.

Fortunately, the same senior teacher who tapped her hand to stop her from speaking before replied, "Sometimes, it's easier to appeal to the male ego." She further explained that as long as she had been there, they always had a male principal. Some of them were open to suggestions, while some only wanted to share their ideas and rarely listened to the teachers. The teachers agreed to allow the principal to tell them what to do so they would never appear to be insubordinate.

Amy shared that she was taught women have an equal voice to men; her mother and father encouraged her to speak up for herself. Additionally, Amy sympathized with her team because they had been through some experiences with other male principals who did not take kindly to them offering their suggestions and other feedback. Although she empathized with them, Amy also made it clear that from now on, if they chose not to speak up, she would speak up on behalf of their team.

From that day forward, Amy took special care to write down suggestions and activities her team shared with each other. Whenever the principal walked into ask for updates, she was intentional about sharing their suggestions and activities. Within two years, Amy became the assistant principal. She became known for encouraging teacher voices, which interestingly was something the principal greatly appreciated.

---

In both scenarios, Dr. Hayes and Amy witnessed herd mentality bias in full effect. They also allowed themselves to be part of discussions with which they were very uncomfortable and did not choose to speak up. While Dr. Hayes was a seasoned educator, Amy was not. Their behaviors were not predicated on age, ethnicity, gender, religion, or any other descriptor.

## PAUSE AND PONDER

- How did the two educators in the scenarios demonstrate the cognitive bias known as the herd mentality bias?

- Recall a time when you agreed to certain behaviors and decisions that did not align with your values. How did you feel? Were you nervous, angry, sad, hurt, or unsettled?

- Now, let's focus on students. Remember a time when you made a decision that impacted students due to the opinions and guidance of others without doing your own research. Did that decision impact students in a positive or negative way? How do you think it made them feel?

Initially, both educators' responses, and the lack thereof, were due to wanting to be part of the "herd" and simply go along to get along. Due to their other experiences, conversations with mentors, and experiences outside the school, both decided to eventually share their views in a way that empowered the collective, which essentially impacted students.

# PAUSE AND PONDER

- Think about the situation you recalled earlier, about a time when you agreed to certain behaviors and decisions that did not align with your values. As you reflect on each scenario and think about your own situation, ask yourself what made you go along with the herd. How would it have made you feel to know the decision makers had asked you for feedback and suggestions before you went along with the herd? Would you have still gone along with the herd? Would being asked to share your thoughts have caused you to make a different decision?

- Examine the situation you recalled earlier that involved a decision *you* made that impacted students. What information do you think would have been valuable to support you in making a more equitable decision, one not based on herd mentality bias? Why weren't you open to sharing your views or ideas? How do you think students would have felt knowing you considered them first and spoke up in situations that could negatively or positively impact them? Do you think they would have felt seen, valued, heard, appreciated, and a sense of belonging?

In each scenario, Dr. Hayes and Amy made a conscious decision at first not to speak up. They chose to be silent; they chose to sit and observe even when they knew certain interactions and decisions could potentially cause harm. It is important to understand that although herd mentality is fueled by emotion, it is a decision. We have the power to consciously make decisions that align with our views, values, and best practices for students. We also have the power to consciously make decisions that align with the herd out of fear and the desire to go along to get along.

Either way, as educators, we have power. Our collective voices have power. Our individual voices have power and the potential to impact the collective in ways that are beyond our imagination. For example, Dr. Hayes had no idea that the director of the consulting agency had already arranged for her staff to receive bias training.

Amy had no idea that her speaking up on behalf of her fellow teachers would land her a promotion. Are there things that you need to speak up about? Are you allowing perceptions about your gender, age, ethnicity, ability, or other descriptors to muffle you? If so, do the very thing you are afraid of—speak up, speak clearly, and trust that your voice will be heard and appreciated.

> Our individual voices have power and the potential to impact the collective in ways that are beyond our imagination.

# Tips for Counteracting Herd Mentality Bias

Counteracting any bias begins with taking a breath. When the subconscious mind is at work, we need to take an intentional step back, beginning with a deep breath. Following are some suggestions for counteracting the herd mentality bias.

- Ask yourself, "What is my motivation or what is my why?" Doing this helps ensure that your behavior aligns with your views and values.

- Celebrate yourself for recognizing that your behavior or verbal stance may be in or out of alignment with your views and values. You are now among those who make conscious intentional decisions, instead of agreeing just to agree or pacify others.

- Remember that operating outside of the herd can be difficult; however, sharing your ideas may be the very thing that is needed to support students and cultivate inclusion.

- Research. One of my former mentors used to remind me to fact check. Make sure your actions and words are in alignment with truth and based on best practices.

- Listen to others outside the herd and consider their perspective as well.

- Continue to attend webinars, conferences, and other forms of professional development so you stay abreast of any new research and strategies that enhance student achievement.

- Ask yourself, "Am I going along to get along?" If the answer is *yes*, stop!

- Remember that your age, gender identity, race, ethnicity, ability, sexual orientation, learning style, religion, along with other qualifiers that make us diverse—your thoughts, words, and actions—are important and deserve to be heard. When you follow these other suggestions, especially fact checking and listening to other perspectives, you make more informed decisions, especially when they are outside the herd.

> When we are directly responsible for students' academic success, and we allow that desire to silence us, we do more harm than good.

Le Bon (1895) stated that a "crowd is always intellectually inferior to the isolated individual;" however, "the crowd may, according to circumstances, be better or worse than the individual" (p. 24). The desire for community is natural, but when we are directly responsible for students' academic success, and we allow that desire to silence us, we do more harm than good.

## Next Steps

The "Herd Mentality Bias Observation and Assessment Tool" can help you observe and assess incidences of herd mentality bias happening in the classroom or larger school community and plan next steps. You can use this tool regardless of your role in the school (teacher, administrator, coach, and so on). You can also share this tool with others in the community to obtain their feedback and suggestions. (Refer back to figure 2.2, page 52, for sample responses to an observation and assessment tool.)

# Herd Mentality Bias Observation and Assessment Tool

**Your Role:** _____

**Type of Bias:** Herd Mentality Bias

**Description of Herd Mentality Bias:** A bias that can be broadly defined as the alignment of the thoughts or behaviors of individuals in a group, following the crowd out of a false sense of belonging or out of fear of being left out.

| Questions | Answers |
|---|---|
| What do you observe in the classroom or larger school community related to this bias? | |
| What are some possible impacts on students? | |
| What are some possible solutions? | |
| What are the next steps for accomplishing the solution? | |
| What resources or assistance might be needed? | |

## CHAPTER 4

# Anchoring Bias

*When you know better, you do better.*

—Grandma Hoover C. Kizart

nchoring bias is one of the most widely studied biases. With more than thirteen research-based books and published articles, it first appeared in a paper published in 1974 by Amos Tversky and Daniel Kahneman, titled *Judgment Under Uncertainty: Heuristics and Biases.* Tversky and Kahneman (1974) describe *anchoring bias* as a cognitive bias "whereby an individual's decisions are influenced by a particular reference point or 'anchor,' which is usually the first information they receive" (p. 1124). Further, they conclude that anchoring bias is often due to the retrievability of instances, which means that we often make decisions based on the availability of information or what we know in the moment.

This can be either good or bad. However, when decisions are anchored in the first piece of information that's available—and there is more to learn, but we do not seek additional information before deciding—it can deter us from making the right decision. This is especially true when students are involved.

For example, when I taught sixth grade, I had a student (I will call her Shana) who often acted disrespectfully. Her tone of voice and the harsh statements she made in class resulted in her being removed from one sixth-grade class and placed in mine. One day, after Shana cursed at another student, I called her mother to discuss my concerns about Shana's behavior. Shana's mother quickly asked me to give her daughter the phone. When Shana took the phone, I heard her mother yell at her and use profane language strong enough to make an adult run for cover. I quickly regretted calling her. When Shana got off the phone, she turned and put her head on my shoulder and cried. As tears rolled down her face, all I could do was console her. The same student who behaved so inappropriately and was incredibly harsh to other students was not that tough at all. Shana's behavior at school reflected what she was experiencing at home.

Instead of shaming her, I began to work with Shana on learning how to communicate with clarity and a cool head. I shared with her the adage that my grandmother taught us: *There is a time and a place for everything.* Over time, Shana started to catch herself before saying hurtful things in class. Instead of flying off the handle, she would take deep breaths, as we practiced, and choose different words to express frustration. By witnessing the interaction between Shana and her mother, I was able to expand my understanding of how Shana showed up in class. She was not just a student with bad behavior, a judgment to which I initially anchored my thoughts. She was a very bright student who began to soar academically, especially in creative writing. I learned firsthand that people are more than the stories we anchor to.

> People are more than the stories we anchor to.

Tversky and Kahneman (1974) also explained anchoring bias as a cognitive shortcut to discovery and problem solving that our brain relies on to assist in decision making. This type of bias is considered a heuristic principle that "reduces the complex task of assessing probabilities and predicting values to simpler judgmental operations" (Tversky & Kahneman, 1974, p. 1124). In other words, when we are in the process of deciding, the brain often creates shortcuts. It can take a shortcut and anchor to the first piece of information it knows, which sometimes leads to severe and systematic errors (Tversky & Kahneman, 1974).

# The Anchoring Effect

In 2022, Yi Zong and Xiaojie Guo expanded the body of research on anchoring bias with a new term, *anchoring effect*, which explains the lens through which we use information to anchor. In their book *An Experimental Study on Anchoring Effect of Consumers' Price Judgment Based on Consumers' Experiencing Scenes*, Zong and

Guo (2022) explain nine factors that influence the anchoring effect. Although their research focuses on anchoring as it connects to the financial market and consumerism, there are clear implications in their work that apply to education. These factors, along with their connection to biases in education, are as follows.

1. **Value:** Consumers anchor and make biased price estimations based on perceived value (Zong & Guo, 2022).

    ¤ *Connection to bias in education:* Educators may make decisions based on a student's perceived value.

2. **Gender:** Consumers make price judgments based on emotion and representation (Zong & Guo, 2022).

    ¤ *Connection to bias in education:* Educators may make biased decisions based on their perceptions of a person's gender, beliefs about gender norms, and emotional connection to a situation.

3. **Emotion:** Consumers make biased price judgments based on their emotional state or mood. When consumers are in a positive emotional state, they tend to be more strongly influenced by the anchoring effect than consumers in a negative emotional state. Those in a negative emotional state may be more critical or judgmental when making decisions (Zong & Guo, 2022).

    ¤ *Connection to bias in education:* An educator's mood or emotional state can impact the decisions they make.

4. **Personality:** Consumers who tend to get along well with others are often highly agreeable and not as suspicious as those who are more difficult to get along with and less agreeable (Zong & Guo, 2022).

    ¤ *Connection to bias in education:* Educators who are highly agreeable tend to anchor more than those who are difficult to get along with because of their suspicious nature.

5. **Expert knowledge and skill:** Consumers often make price judgments based on their knowledge of a product and are more strongly influenced by the anchoring effect when making purchasing decisions (Zong & Guo, 2022).

    ¤ *Connection to bias in education:* Educators who have less knowledge and experience may tend to make more anchoring-biased decisions than those who have more knowledge and experience.

6.  **Time pressure:** Consumer experience is affected by time limitations and the time frame in which decisions are made. This impacts the judgments and perceptions consumers have about products (Zong & Guo, 2022).

    ¤  *Connection to bias in education:* The time of day as well as the amount of pressure we feel that we must make a decision may cause educators to make anchoring-biased decisions.

7.  **Early warning indication:** Consumers are more objective in making decisions when they have information about a product in advance (Zong & Guo, 2022).

    ¤  *Connection to bias in education:* Having additional time and receiving information prior to weighing in on decisions that impact students aids in minimizing anchoring bias.

8.  **Cognitive need:** Consumers with high cognitive needs often think and reflect before making decisions. They also ask more questions and seek truth because of their desire to understand the world around them. Conversely, consumers with lower cognitive needs are more influenced by the anchoring effect because they tend to rely on their past knowledge and aren't as open to new information (Zong & Guo, 2022).

    ¤  *Connection to bias in education:* Educators who rely on their prior knowledge of a student, policy, or practice are more susceptible to anchoring bias than those who are intrinsically motivated to learn and ask questions to assist in making informed, nonbiased decisions.

9.  **Self-confidence level:** Consumers with high self-confidence make biased decisions based on the anchoring effect because they are certain of their own knowledge and judgments (Zong & Guo, 2022).

> Holding too tightly to one idea, policy, or procedure can result in stagnation or ineffective decisions because we don't allow ourselves to receive new information that can inform decision making.

    ¤  *Connection to bias in education:* Educators with high self-efficacy and self-confidence are prone to anchoring bias because they seek to confirm what they already know.

Other researchers (Lee & Morewedge, 2022; Von Hecker, Klauer, & Aßfalg, 2019; Zhou & Shen, 2021) confirm that anchoring bias impacts decision-making processes. Holding too tightly to one idea, policy, or procedure can result in stagnation or ineffective decisions. Just as consumers in business and retail are anchored because of the psychological changes some avoid when making decisions, educators and administrators might do the same.

# Bias Assessment

Use the checklist in figure 4.1 to assess your own anchoring bias and check for understanding of this specific cognitive bias. As you respond to each descriptor, remember to be honest and give yourself grace. This is an opportunity to see yourself more clearly so you can respond in a way that prevents the negative impacts of anchoring bias in your school. Following the checklist are two scenarios that will assist in expanding your knowledge of how this bias shows up in schools.

| Descriptor | Most of the Time | Sometimes | Never |
|---|---|---|---|
| It is easy for me to listen to the knowledge and expertise of others. | | | |
| I feel uncomfortable when I am among other educators who I think know more than me. | | | |
| I intentionally seek new learning opportunities on a regular basis by listening to podcasts, reading literature, listening to a variety of news sources, and so on. | | | |
| I feel comfortable when someone expresses a different opinion from my own. | | | |
| I feel uncomfortable or challenged when others express different opinions from my own. | | | |

**FIGURE 4.1:** Anchoring bias self-reflection checklist.

continued →

| Descriptor | Most of the Time | Sometimes | Never |
|---|---|---|---|
| I take my time to consider all sides of a situation before making a decision, especially when it involves my least favorite students. | | | |
| I tend to lean on prior knowledge and experience when dealing with students, especially those whom I usually consider troublemakers. | | | |
| I tend to lean on prior knowledge and experience when dealing with students with whom I have favorable relationships. | | | |
| I am objective when making decisions that impact students. | | | |
| I take my time to consider all sides of the situation before making a decision. | | | |
| When I am feeling time pressure, I usually step back to allow myself time to decompress and consider all the information I have before making a decision. | | | |
| When I feel pressed for time, I usually make decisions based on what I already know about the situation or student. | | | |
| I am aware that sometimes my thoughts about gender roles impact my decision making regarding students. | | | |
| I realize there are certain times of the day I am more effective and able to make more objective decisions than other times of the day. | | | |
| I have a trusted mentor or seasoned educator who helps me expand my knowledge so I can make more informed decisions. | | | |

Reflect on your answers. Consider the following questions to guide your reflections.

1. What makes it easy or difficult for me to listen to the expertise of others?

2. How do I respond when someone's opinion challenges my own beliefs?

3. How can I improve my ability to stay objective with students I find difficult?

4. How do my prior knowledge and experiences shape my interactions with students, especially those whom I may deem as troublemakers?

5. What are the potential risks of making decisions based solely on past knowledge?

Now that you have taken your personal inventory, read the following scenarios, which illustrate the impact of anchoring bias in schools. After reading each scenario, revisit the checklist to reevaluate your answers.

# Scenario 1

Trustee Elementary School was a charter school in a rural community located in North Dakota. For more than a decade, the school built a reputation of being elite based on high accolades for their overall mathematics scores in grades K–5. This, coupled with the fact that the governor's daughter attended Trustee Elementary, caused people to believe that it was one of the best schools in the state. The news media seemed to cover every great thing that happened at the school, so parents came from near and far to enroll their students. Parents were also very involved in the PTA and attended board meetings regularly.

During a parent meeting held in late May, Mr. Oaks, the parent of a third-grade student, commented that his child's reading scores were lower than the state average. This was the first time any of the elementary school students took the standardized state assessment. He wanted to know if other third-grade students scored low on the statewide test as well. As he and other parents began to discuss more about their children's scores, they became concerned about the quality of literacy instruction students were receiving across grade levels. Because this was a relatively small community, most of the parents knew each other. They also had close relationships with some of the teachers, so they knew exactly with whom to share their concerns. One of the parents decided to call in a third-grade teacher to ask about the reading scores.

Parents were surprised to hear that reading scores were low for most of the students in grades K–5, and that the school recently hired a literacy coach. The literacy coach was tasked with working with teachers to help improve their pedagogy, the way they taught reading comprehension. Literacy coaches also met with students to provide supplemental support to strengthen their reading comprehension skills to get them on grade level. Parents were upset to find out that so many students in third grade were reading below grade level. This did not align with their impression of the school.

While some parents decided to invest in tutors outside of Trustee Elementary to provide support for their children in reading comprehension, others met with the principal and demanded new teachers. Parents were frustrated they had not known about the students' low reading scores. They gave too much attention to the mathematics accolades and the reputation of the school based on the media. Parents also thought that since the governor's daughter attended Trustee Elementary, all was well, so they did not notice other important issues like the quality of literacy instruction. As the literacy coach worked with the school, and some new teachers were hired, the school began to earn accolades for both mathematics and reading.

# Scenario 2

Enrique Gonzalez was a teacher who truly enjoyed teaching. Being a teacher at Hummingbird Middle School was one of his lifetime dreams. He enjoyed watching students learn and stretched their thinking on subjects of which they had little to no understanding before entering his class. Mr. Gonzalez also enjoyed planning special events for all the middle school students to celebrate milestones and achievements. He was very engaged in several committees at the middle school and aspired to become an assistant principal.

He loved everything about his job except for being one of the only men in the building. Like most schools in the district, the majority of teachers and administrators were women. He noticed that often, he and the other male teachers or counselors in the building were asked to intervene in disciplinary issues. He was also often asked to supervise after-school detention during times other meetings or school activities were planned.

Mr. Gonzalez had little to no experience in dealing with behavioral issues. Outside of the strategies he learned in college and additional professional development given to all classroom teachers, he did not have additional qualifications to justify why he was always the one teachers and administrators called to intervene in disciplinary issues and supervising after-school detention. Some teachers jokingly referred to him as the "school disciplinarian." They relied on him to get the students straight, especially the male students.

Mr. Gonzalez resented being referred to as the school disciplinarian. Often, other teachers and administrators would call him out of class to speak to a student who was having disciplinary issues in other classes. This upset Mr. Gonzalez for years, because he took pride in his ability to differentiate learning for his students, not in scolding or policing them during detention. He began to question why he, of all teachers, was expected to take on the additional duties of school disciplinarian.

His mentor, another male teacher at a different school, encouraged him to talk with the administrators to let them know he did not want to take on what he considered a burden that was not shared by other teachers. Mr. Gonzalez strongly believed he was called to be the disciplinarian because he was one of the few men in the school building.

One day, Mr. Gonzalez made an appointment to speak with the administrators about his concerns. Both female administrators confirmed they relied on him because he was a man to whom they felt students would listen because of his tall stature and presence. The assistant principal even went on to say students were afraid of him, so they used that as leverage to get them in line.

This concerned Mr. Gonzalez because that was not his purpose for being a teacher. He explained he had a knack for planning activities and would like to invest more time doing things that celebrated student achievement. He also took the advice of his mentor and told them he was concerned that he was being asked to serve as a disciplinarian for the school because he was a man. He asked that the other teachers share the responsibility of supervising after-school detention. Mr. Gonzalez also shared that he didn't want students to fear him and explained that constantly being taken away from class to help solve disciplinary issues was preventing him from fully engaging his own class and distracted him from his primary goal—teaching. Mr. Gonzalez explained that he believed other teachers were just as capable of handling disciplinary issues and asked them to give others a chance.

The principal and assistant principal apologized to Mr. Gonzalez. They decided to have a rotating schedule that included all teachers in supervising after-school detention. Additionally, they stopped disturbing him during class to intervene in issues concerning students in other classes. After a while, other teachers did the same. He was able to focus more on teaching and planning activities and awards for students to encourage good behavior.

In both scenarios, anchoring bias caused parents and educators to make decisions that unfortunately impacted students. In the first scenario, parents learned a hard lesson about anchoring the first piece of information they received about schools. I have witnessed this go both ways. Sometimes, parents might anchor information about a school based on its location without thoroughly investigating the academic rigor and extracurricular activities that encourage schools as community. In the second scenario, the fact that there were not many male teachers in the building made Mr. Gonzalez an anomaly. As a male teacher, people anchored to their assumptions that he was a good disciplinarian. Interestingly, there may have been other teachers who were better suited to ensure the rules of the school were obeyed, but they weren't given a chance possibly due to anchoring bias related to gender roles.

# PAUSE AND PONDER

- How did these two scenarios demonstrate the cognitive bias known as anchoring bias?

- Think back to a time when you experienced a decision being made based on a widespread or popular belief because someone was anchored in their views about gender roles, race, disability, or other characteristics. How did this decision impact you? How did you feel knowing that a decision was made only using prior knowledge or ideas based on first impressions and beliefs? Were you angry, sad, hurt, or unsettled?

- Now, let's focus on students. Remember a time when you made a decision that impacted students because you were anchored to your views about them. Did you base your decision on prior knowledge or widespread beliefs about them? Did you do your due diligence to ensure you asked questions and gathered additional information to assist you with making a non-anchoring-biased decision that would impact them? How did you know you were anchoring to views, ideas, old information, or beliefs about the students? How do you think it made them feel?

# Tips for Counteracting Anchoring Bias

Again, counteracting any bias begins with taking a breath. Intentional pauses and deep breaths allow us to take a step back so we can think about our thinking as opposed to making decisions based on our first thought. The following are some suggestions for counteracting anchoring bias.

> Anchoring is the brain's way of taking shortcuts when making decisions. Refuse to take the easy way out.

- As you take a deep breath, ask yourself, "What is the decision that needs to be made?" Doing this helps ensure you are clear about information you need to consider to make more informed decisions.

- Remember that anchoring is the brain's way of taking shortcuts when making decisions. Refuse to take the easy way out.

- Research! Consider each decision you must make carefully and with the presence of mind to consider each decision with an open mind . . . . and heart. If it involves a student, ask yourself if you have heard all sides of the story objectively. If it involves a student you don't like (let's keep it real . . . we've all encountered students who we find very challenging and merely tolerate), bring in another adult or ask for input from a coworker or administrator who is emotionally neutral with the student.

- If there is a policy decision you must make, be sure to diversify the committee of people who weigh in on any changes. This helps ensure there are differences of thoughts and perspectives that can expand our knowledge base to make more informed decisions.

- Intentionally listen to different podcasts or independent news sources to learn from a variety of perspectives on a regular basis.

- Ask yourself, "Do I know all that I need to know to make a fair and equitable decision?" If the answer is *no*, seek more information before making a decision. Sometimes taking extra time to make decisions helps ensure that we consider other perspectives and new knowledge.

- Celebrate yourself for recognizing that you may need to learn or consider before deciding.

- Consider your own thoughts about gender roles, race, ethnicity, ability, gender identity, sexual orientation, learning style, religion, and other qualifiers that make us diverse. Don't allow your views about others who appear to be the same or different to color your decisions. As Sharroky Hollie told me during his Cultural Language Academy of Success training, "Don't let your first thought be your last thought" (S. Hollie, personal communication, September 15, 2019).

- Get a mentor. A trusted mentor or colleague is helpful to have at all stages of your career. They can help provide you with different perspectives based on knowledge or lived experiences that can help inform your decisions.

- Avoid toxic positivity—that is, saying things are OK when they really aren't. If you are not in the mood, take a moment (or two) to collect yourself emotionally before making a decision.

- Remember, we are all valuable. Most of us have someone in our lives who loves us. Consider the golden rule of "treat people like you want to be treated," and treat people like you want one of your loved ones to be treated. Gather and consider all the information you would want someone to include if they were making a decision that impacted you or someone you love.

- Remember, it's OK not to know. Relieve yourself of the pressure we often put on ourselves to know everything regarding students, the school community, and job responsibilities. We are all works in progress.

> We are all works
> in progress.

Anchoring bias, or anchoring effect, is one of the many biases that can impede our ability to make well-informed decisions. We are all works in progress. Conversely, when we do not take the time to gather all necessary information or simply make decisions based on prior knowledge of a student or situation, our decision making can be flawed.

# Next Steps

The "Anchoring Bias Observation and Assessment Tool" (page 84) can help you observe and assess incidences of anchoring bias happening in the classroom or larger school community, and plan next steps. You can use this tool regardless of your role in the school (teacher, administrator, coach, and so on). You can also share this tool with others in the community to obtain their feedback and suggestions. (Refer back to figure 2.2, page 52, for sample responses to an observation and assessment tool.)

# Anchoring Bias Observation and Assessment Tool

**Your Role:** _____

**Type of Bias:** Anchoring Bias

**Description of Anchoring Bias:** A bias involving anchoring or holding on to information we know, which is usually based on prior knowledge, when making decisions. This cognitive shortcut causes us to rely solely on what we already know or to seek information that validates the thoughts and ideas to which we are anchored.

| Questions | Answers |
|---|---|
| What do you observe in the classroom or larger school community related to this bias? | |
| What are some possible impacts on students? | |
| What are some possible solutions? | |
| What are the next steps for accomplishing the solution? | |
| What resources or assistance might be needed? | |

## CHAPTER 5

# Decision Fatigue Bias

*Avoid making irrevocable decisions while tired or hungry.*

—Robert A. Heinlein

ike many educators, I am also a parent. In my role as a parent, I sometimes feel overwhelmed by the number of decisions I have to make throughout the day. Combined with the responsibilities I have in my career, and others as a daughter, sister, philanthropist, community organizer, writer, and devout lover of nature walks, the number of decisions I make in a day can be daunting.

I'm sure this sounds familiar to many administrators, teachers, and other education professionals. I've noticed I make more clear-headed decisions during the early part of my day than I do toward the latter part. If I'm being completely honest, I also get a little cantankerous toward the end of the day, especially Monday through Friday when I have prepared breakfast, picked up my children from school, worked through the majority of my to-do list for work, made dinner, and so on. While one might say this is simply a function of being overwhelmed, research on decision fatigue bias explains how the brain takes cognitive shortcuts that can impact not only our personal relationships but also our school communities.

## Depletion and Decision Fatigue

In late 1998, Roy Baumeister, Ellen Bratslavsky, Mark Muraven, and Dianne Tice researched and published an article about ego depletion titled *Ego Depletion: Is the*

*Active Self a Limited Resource?* They define *ego depletion* as "acts of volition drawn on some limited resource" (Baumeister et al., 1998, p. 1252). Their research explained that human beings are equipped with free will and a sense of independence that enables them to make various types of decisions. This free will, coupled with the wide variety of decisions human beings make on a day-to-day basis, can be influenced by "low-lying urges" or "higher-order reasoning." In their research on ego depletion, they describe these terms as follows.

> We are frequently faced with a choice between obeying our basic, low-lying urges (eating a piece of cake, sleeping in, venting our anger, etc.), or suppressing them with higher order, more reasonable choices, favoring long-term benefits (eating healthy, going to work, or biting our tongue). (Baumeister et al., 1998, p. 1253)

Additionally, they concluded that decisions can be impacted by three factors: (1) mood, (2) diet, and (3) fatigue and the desire to quit (Baumeister et al., 1998). Both the low-lying urges and higher-order, more reasonable choices are impacted by our mental dexterity, which can be altered as our energy, a "vital resource of the self" becomes depleted (Baumeister et al., 1998, p. 1264).

In 2011, Baumeister extended his studies with fellow psychologist John Tierney and published their work in the book *Willpower* by dedicating an entire chapter to decision fatigue. They analyzed more than six hundred studies about decision making, including shopping for tailored suits and new cars, forming relationships, and so on. They found a common link between the way people make decisions and how many decisions they make during the day.

> Once willpower is depleted, people are less able to make solid, good decisions.

In summary, they concluded that decision making depletes willpower. Once willpower is depleted, people are less able to make solid, good decisions. When we are in positions that require us to make decisions all day long, we may begin to feel depleted and start looking for ways to conserve energy, finding excuses to avoid or postpone decisions. Decision fatigue bias can cause us to look for the easiest and safest options (Baumeister & Tierney, 2011).

When I first started teaching, I heard fellow educators talk about teacher burnout and grading fatigue. They used these terms to describe how they were feeling after repetitious tasks, like grading, or when overwhelmed by the various responsibilities that come along with being an educator. These are all functions of decision fatigue bias caused by mental exhaustion.

The cognitive shortcuts we take when we are exhausted or engaged in repetitious tasks make decision fatigue one of the most problematic biases discussed in this book. We not only impact students when we are depleted, but our health is also affected. In other words, when we take cognitive shortcuts that can dilute the executive function of our brain, it can lead to "irrational" decisions (Baumeister et al., 1998; Baumeister & Tierney, 2011; Brownlee, 2020).

After my fifth year of teaching, I decided I wanted to be a principal. One of our graduate school assignments was to shadow three principals. All the principals I was assigned to observe had excellent reputations and were stellar leaders. While I shadowed them, I noticed their interactions with students, staff, board members, and families. I also observed the way they did or did not prioritize their health.

It appeared that the success and failure of a school rested on the principal's shoulders. The hours were long and included weekend events as well as notorious "other duties as assigned." I saw firsthand how principals would forget not only to eat but also take breaks. Each principal I observed had one thing in common. Toward the latter half of the day, they made quicker decisions. Sometimes, they were even more quick tempered. They did not consider all the aspects of a given situation later in the day as they did prior to lunchtime.

Something about navigating all the various moving parts during the students' lunchtime that drained each principal afterward. One principal exhibited decision fatigue when they suspended a student for three days; earlier, another student received in school detention for the same infraction. Because I was there to learn, I asked if there was a difference between the students. I was wondering if one often got in more trouble than the other. Their response was, "I'm just too tired to figure this out right now."

Another principal I observed excessively reprimanded one student while allowing another with the same infraction to get away with a simple lecture (a scenario you will read about later in this chapter). I was interim principal for three months when I realized the position was too stressful for me to entertain. Hats off to all principals and other administrators reading this book! This is a great example of how we all have different capabilities, skills, and talents. Where one person may have the bandwidth to navigate as an administrator, that same person may not have the wherewithal to be a kindergarten teacher. Our differences, as it relates to our skills, talents, and abilities, are important to note, especially when making career choices. I wonder if trying to fit ourselves into roles we do not have the bandwidth or passion for adds to decision fatigue.

> I wonder if trying to fit ourselves into roles we do not have the bandwidth or passion for adds to decision fatigue.

## Bias Assessment

Use the checklist in figure 5.1 to assess your own decision fatigue bias and check for understanding of this specific cognitive bias. As you reflect on each descriptor, indicate the frequency you relate to each statement. Remember to be honest and give yourself grace. This is an opportunity to see yourself more clearly so you can respond in a way that prevents the negative impacts of decision fatigue bias in your school. Following the checklist are two scenarios that will assist in expanding your knowledge of how this bias shows up in schools.

| Descriptor | Most of the Time | Sometimes | Never |
| --- | --- | --- | --- |
| During the course of the day, I tend to make a lot of decisions. Consider personal, family, and work decisions. | | | |
| I am overwhelmed by too many choices. | | | |
| I feel confused when approached with too many options. | | | |
| I avoid major decision-making tasks. | | | |
| There are times during the day when I feel overwhelmed. | | | |
| I use intentional strategies when I feel overwhelmed. | | | |
| I experience brain fog, the inability to think clearly. | | | |

| | | | |
|---|---|---|---|
| I often juggle multiple tasks. | | | |
| I consider myself a procrastinator. | | | |
| I am short tempered when approached with too many decisions to make at once. | | | |
| I feel irritated when I have a lot of decisions to make. | | | |
| I put off tasks that require me to make decisions that will impact others. | | | |
| I tend to take a long time to make decisions. | | | |
| When I make decisions, I feel dissatisfied or wonder if I made the correct choice. | | | |
| I experience headaches or tension in my body when making a lot of decisions. | | | |
| I tend to skip lunch during the day to maximize productivity. | | | |
| I rarely take regular work breaks to replenish my energy. | | | |
| I ask for help when I feel overwhelmed. | | | |
| My list of priorities often gets thrown off because of the number of decisions I must make during the course of the day. | | | |
| I intentionally organize my week to make room for self-care such as rest, exercise, and eating. | | | |

Reflect on your answers. Consider the following questions to guide your reflections.

1. What types of decisions do I find myself making most frequently in each area of my life (personal, family, work)?

2. How do I typically respond when I feel overwhelmed by multiple options, especially if I am fatigued?

3. What time of day do I usually make the best decisions? Conversely, what time of day am I usually physically, emotionally, or mentally fatigued?

4. How do I typically cope with feelings of being overwhelmed, especially when I have to keep going because I am at work with students?

5. How does brain fog impact my productivity and decision-making abilities?

**FIGURE 5.1:** Decision fatigue bias self-reflection checklist.

*Visit **go.SolutionTree.com/diversityandequity** for a free reproducible version of this figure.*

Now that you have taken your personal inventory, read the following scenarios, which illustrate the impact of decision fatigue bias in schools. After reading each scenario, revisit the checklist to reevaluate your answers.

# Scenario 1

Principal Edwards was one of the most well-respected administrators in the Tealwood School District. She worked as a teacher, instructional coach, guidance counselor, and assistant before serving as a principal. Teachers came to her for guidance with academics and a variety of other issues. She was well-liked by teachers and fellow administrators.

Principal Edwards enjoyed assisting teachers with strategies that helped students improve academically. However, her new position as an administrator came with additional responsibilities. Managing staff, school activities, and class schedules, and creating a culture of inclusion that maintained curriculum standards and student discipline were new responsibilities. Of all the new tasks for which she was now responsible, student discipline was her least favorite.

Because she was once a guidance counselor, she had great empathy for many students, because she knew the reasons many of them struggled socially and academically in class. Her role as a guidance counselor allowed her to provide strategies to students to assist them when they were having difficulty. As principal, her role was a bit different, because any school suspension had to come through her for approval. She did not look forward to this responsibility, as she did not believe sending students home would solve anything.

Through the course of her trajectory as an educator, she saw many students get suspended and come back to school with the same behavior. Sometimes, their behavior was even worse. Her experience as a guidance counselor was directly in conflict with one of the responsibilities of this new role as school principal. Still, when teachers sent office referrals to her, Principal Edwards and her assistant principal reviewed them and listened to all sides of the stories before making recommendations.

Principal Edwards noticed that some of the same students were regulars in her office. Because of budget cuts, there was no longer a guidance counselor designated for her building. The district had one guidance counselor who was responsible for assisting all the K–12 students. Principal Edwards knew this was a difficult and sometimes impossible task, so she often took on the role of guidance counselor for many students who frequently got in trouble. So now, she was serving as an unofficial instructional coach for four teachers, the unofficial guidance counselor, and principal with additional duties for which she was still responsible. Her office was always busy.

When Principal Edwards noticed she had started losing weight, she attributed it to stress. The stress of being everything to everyone in the school was starting to take its toll on her health. She figured she could manage this by taking small breaks throughout the day, but if a student was sent to her office or a teacher dropped in for advice during her planned break, she would forget to take a moment for herself and focus instead on their needs. After a while, this became a regular pattern. Principal Edwards was the first to arrive in the morning and last to leave.

One morning, a student was sent to her office because he was caught drawing on the wall in one of the hallways. This form of school vandalism is immediately punishable by school suspension; however, since it was the student's first infraction, Principal Edwards decided that having the student clean up his drawing was punishment enough. As the day continued, she did not take a break, as usual. She had back-to-back meetings with several teachers, curriculum meetings, another student who drew on the walls who was given the same consequence to clean it up, and a two-hour-long district administrator meeting.

Right before dismissal, a student was sent to the office with a referral because he wrote on his desk. Principal Edwards told the student she was fed up with him vandalizing school property. She went on to suspend the student for two days and told him he needed to clean the writing off the desk before he left. She called the student's parents to let them know their child would be staying after school to clean the desk and that he was suspended for two days. Although the parents agreed their child needed to take responsibility for his behavior, they also expressed concern that suspension was harsh for a first-time reprimand.

Principal Edwards went home later that evening and explained the situation to her sister, who was also an educator. She vented, saying she was tired of students thinking they could vandalize the school and get away with it. Her sister listened and asked her a very simple question: "Why did the other students who were caught drawing on the hallway walls not get suspended like the student who was caught drawing on his desk?" Her sister, who was familiar with bias and its impact on our decision making, jokingly asked, "Did you not like the student you suspended?" She simply wanted to understand why there was such a significant difference between the consequences for all three students.

Principal Edwards explained that she was familiar with all three students and thought they were brilliant. When her sister suggested that she was too tired at the end of the day, Principal Edwards immediately regretted her decision. She also admitted that she didn't know how to make it right.

The sisters talked about the importance of balance. Principal Edwards decided that going forward, she would keep her open-door policy; however, she would ask her administrative assistant to secure at least two ten-minute breaks throughout the day. She would also take healthy snacks with her to school, along with a bottle of water, to ensure she ate throughout the day.

Principal Edwards also decided she would be more intentional about referring students to the district's guidance counselor so she could free herself from some of that responsibility. Last, she decided to arrange a meeting with the three students and their parents who were caught drawing and writing on school property. Admittedly, she feared the students and parents would be angry that one student was treated differently from the other two. Just as she encouraged students to practice integrity and take responsibility for their actions, she thought it was important for her to do the same.

The parents of the student who was suspended were upset. But after Principal Edwards explained that she made an error due to being exhausted, and she would reverse the school suspension, the conversation shifted, and it became a teachable moment for everyone in the meeting. The students learned that writing on school property was not acceptable. They also learned that when they make a mistake, it is good to admit it, make amends, and move forward. Principal Edwards was responsible for that lesson. Additionally, the parents acknowledged that they often made decisions because they were tired and empathized with Principal Edwards.

The parents gained a great deal of respect for Principal Edwards and advocated for the school board to provide more guidance counselors for students throughout the school district. Principal Edwards kept her word to herself and made a conscious point throughout the day to take breaks in between meetings and decisions. She also arranged a teacher in-service during their next professional development day on biases, including decision fatigue bias.

# Scenario 2

Dr. McGregor was a retired English professor who spent most of his career at Obatala University. He loved working with students and supporting them with their creative writing. He started his teaching career in higher education in his late twenties after finishing his doctoral degree. Dr. McGregor was the author of several books and the editor of a nationally published journal with no desire to be an administrator, superintendent, or, in his words, "anyone with any governing power." Students loved the type of assignments he gave in class as well as the way he encouraged them to think outside the box. However, many students also complained about his unfair grading practices, stating they weren't consistent. On some days, assignments were graded very loosely, but on other days, students were penalized for mistakes that were overlooked on earlier assignments.

Dr. McGregor did not understand why students felt that way. He settled into the understanding that he couldn't please everyone, so he kept moving forward year after year in the same way, with some students OK with his grading practices while others expressed disappointment. This went on throughout his career in higher education.

After working more than thirty years as an English professor, he decided he still had the energy to work. He decided to share his love of creative writing with high school students at a neighborhood school. His start as a high school teacher was an opportunity for him to reinvent himself and share his love for creative writing while also developing a new reputation for himself. Specifically, Dr. McGregor was a stickler for punctuation in creative writing. Like all teachers, he gave students assignments throughout the school year that helped them practice the skills they already had while also implementing new skills.

Throughout the year, he assigned various types of creative writing papers students enjoyed. Many students commented that they appreciated the opportunity to express their thoughts creatively. The only complaint students had was how he graded spelling and punctuation. Some students felt that, in creative writing, there were spelling and punctuation rules that should not apply because it stifled their creativity. Other students complained he graded some papers differently than others. Dr. McGregor addressed these concerns by sharing with students that even creatives had to follow certain rules. He thought students were just complaining because they didn't want to follow those rules. He remembered being a student and complaining about almost anything concerning school. So, once again, he did not give a thought to students' complaints, especially because most of them did a great job with assignments.

Marybeth was one of Dr. McGregor's stellar students. She was always in class, submitted assignments on time, and was applauded for creativity in her stories. One day, she met with Dr. McGregor after class to discuss her grade on a recent assignment. She noted that on a prior assignment, he didn't take off points for spelling and punctuation the same way that he did on her current assignment. She was frustrated because he deducted a point for every misspelled word and every punctuation mistake. He wanted to give Marybeth the benefit of the doubt, so he asked to see her other papers. After studying a few of her other graded assignments he too noticed some inconsistencies. Admittedly, he did not understand why he had graded some of the papers differently than others. So, he decided to alter the grade on Marybeth's current paper to address the more immediate concern.

As time went on, he noticed that while grading papers, he had developed a habit of penalizing spelling and grammar more heavily on the papers he graded first. He realized that, after grading stacks and stacks of creative writing essays, he became more lackadaisical in his grading process. Once he noticed this, he wanted to understand what he could do to change it. As luck would have it, in a staff meeting, one of his colleagues shared an article about decision fatigue bias in grading. He was glad to learn that this was a common concern among teachers. However, he wanted to ensure he didn't continue making the same mistake.

To assist him with grading papers more equitably, he developed a rubric and shared it with students. Spelling and punctuation were still categories that were heavily weighted. However, having a rubric helped to ensure his grading practices were fair regardless of how many piles of papers he had to grade.

In both scenarios, educators who were otherwise extraordinary in their field had challenges because of decision fatigue. Principal Edwards, as someone who had a lot of experience and respect from other educators, was challenged by being overwhelmed by multiple tasks involving students. She was so used to mentoring and supporting teachers as a former instructional coach that she often assumed that role, as well. Being a new administrator had its own set of challenges. She allowed other educators to pull on her, which caused her to feel overwhelmed, so much so that she often unintentionally made inequitable decisions.

Similarly, Dr. McGregor was overwhelmed by repetitious tasks, which led to inequitable grading practices. As a former classroom teacher, I can relate to being overwhelmed by the daunting task of grading mountains of papers. What about you?

# PAUSE AND PONDER

- How did the two educators in the scenarios demonstrate decision fatigue bias?

- Recall a time when you observed someone making a decision while they were tired, fatigued, or overwhelmed. How did this decision impact you or someone else? How did you feel knowing a decision was made from a space of fatigue or wanting to just be done with the decision at hand? If it were you making the decision, did you regret your choice? If you were observing the decision being made, how did you feel knowing the decision was not being made under optimal conditions?

- Now, let's focus on students. Recognize a time you made a decision when you were fatigued. How did you know your

continued →

decision impacted students? How do you think it made them feel, and what else could you have done?

Sometimes, we are appointed to positions in which we are required to wear multiple hats. Other times, like Principal Edwards, we wear multiple hats because of experience and our inability to say no or set appropriate boundaries to allow for change that could lead to being less overwhelmed. Additionally, like with Dr. McGregor, sometimes repetitious actions can cause us to become careless or overwhelmed. Dr. McGregor clearly had a system of grading to which he was so accustomed, he did not realize the mistakes he was making while grading, thus impacting students' grades both negatively and positively. Fortunately for both the students and the two educators, they had enough integrity and took the personal responsibility to correct their mistakes.

# PAUSE AND PONDER

- As you reflect on each scenario and think about your own situation, ask yourself what else could you have done. How would it have made you feel to know everyone was rested and making the decision when they were at their best? Would you have felt grateful they respected themselves and you enough to make decisions while at their best? Would you have felt valued and appreciated?

- Examine the situation you recalled earlier that involved a decision *you* made that impacted students. How could resting, eating, staying hydrated, and other self-care methods have helped you make a more equitable decision? Why were you tired? Were you taking care of yourself in the best way you know how? How do you think students would have felt knowing you made decisions while you were at the top of your game, your best self? Do you think they would have felt valued and appreciated?

In both scenarios, the educators made a classic mistake, a mistake many of us make every day. Overworking and overtaxing ourselves leads to decision fatigue bias. They both took a cognitive shortcut caused by this bias. Principal Edwards decided to suspend a student for an infraction others committed earlier because she was frustrated and tired. Dr. McGregor took the same cognitive shortcut because after heavily grading stacks of papers, grading the remaining papers less stringently seemed like the easiest thing to do. Both of their decisions directly impacted students. Had they not corrected their behavior, it could have gone on for many more years.

Thankfully, the students were very forgiving. However, it must have been difficult for students to suffer grading inequities and "too severe" punishments. I imagine the student who was suspended probably felt terrible, not only for their mistake, but also for the way their mistake was inequitably handled.

Both educators showed integrity and personal responsibility by taking accountability for their mistakes. While students' feelings were negatively impacted, the fact that both adults were able to make amends for those mistakes meant a great deal to students. Using the following strategies could have mitigated the impact of decision fatigue bias for both educators and students.

# Tips for Counteracting Decision Fatigue Bias

Counteracting any bias begins with taking a breath. Intentional pauses and deep breaths allow us to take a step back to consciously process our behaviors. The suggestions for counteracting decision fatigue bias are a bit different from the others in that they involve self-care.

- First and foremost, step back and ask yourself, "Am I tired?" Our bodies need rest. However, sometimes we push ourselves above the limit and don't get the amount of rest we need out of fear that we may not have enough time to complete other tasks. Understand that sleep is a necessity, not a luxury or an option.

- Eat. I can't emphasize this enough. Too often, educators, including administrators, guidance counselors, librarians, and so on, will forgo this basic need for the sake of accomplishing a task. The need to fuel our bodies through food is a *need*, not a luxury or an option. Although this is not a healthy food guidebook, it is important to note that eating healthy foods provides the necessary nutrients your body needs to function well. Educators have high-impact jobs. When we lack nutrients, it impacts our level of fatigue and can cause us to be *hangry* (hungry and angry at the same time). So, if you really want to make a positive impact in education and counteract decision fatigue bias, make a point to stop and eat.

- Hydrate. I won't get all scientific on you. We have all heard how important it is to drink plenty of water! When we deny our bodies the hydration they need, we may be doing ourselves and the students we serve a great disservice. Drinking water throughout the course of the day keeps us hydrated, which leads to making clearer decisions because we are not as fatigued.

- Take breaks between tasks throughout the day. This can be a short, ten-minute break or a longer fifteen- to twenty-minute break, depending on how long you worked on one task and the seriousness of the decisions you need to make later in the day. For example, several years ago, I noticed that one of my mentors, an administrator in higher education, left his office every hour or so. It was noticeable because he was the only administrator who I saw walking around campus a few times throughout the day. One day, after asking him how he finds the time to walk around campus, he replied, "I make time." He went on to explain that he saw a lot of administrators lose themselves and burn out because they didn't take the time to treat themselves as humans first. This, along with other conversations with educators and administrators, helped me conclude that taking breaks is a choice. When we set a precedent with others in our workplace that signals, we are willing to work, work, work with no pause, that becomes the expectation.

- Organize your priorities and make an effort to tend to the most impactful decisions during the time of the day when you are at your best.

- Ask for help. If you notice you are tired, allow others you trust to share the mental load of decision making with you. Sometimes, it takes one trusted colleague or fellow educator to encourage you to have a different perspective on a situation, especially one that involves students.

- Limit yourself to four or five significant choices per day when possible. If this is not possible, follow some of the previously mentioned tips to help ensure you are not making choices from a space of indifference or frustration because you are fatigued.

- Plan your agenda a day in advance so you don't have to make as many decisions in the morning.

- Learn to notice when you are tired, hungry, or dehydrated. Plan to take care of your needs.

- Postpone decisions if you are tired or not at your best. It is better to wait to weigh in on a decision than make one that may negatively impact a student, colleague, or anyone else in the school community.

Decision fatigue bias is like driving while sleepy or intoxicated. The vehicle is still moving, but it may run off the road, or worse yet, hit someone. Being tired is natural when we do not have the necessary nutrients to nurture our bodies. Sometimes, our tendency to cram a lot into the day and the natural occurrence of grading lots of papers can exacerbate mental fatigue.

> Decision fatigue bias is like driving while sleepy or intoxicated.

There are many things you can do to help yourself before you get to a place of fatigue. What is equally important is that once you notice you are fatigued and might not be making the highest cognitive decisions, especially when impacting a student, it becomes your responsibility to take a step back. Follow the strategies in this chapter to help manage decision fatigue bias so you do less harm to yourself and your students.

## Next Steps

The "Decision Fatigue Bias Observation and Assessment Tool" can help you observe and assess incidences of decision fatigue bias happening in the classroom or larger school community and plan next steps. You can use this tool regardless of your role in the school (teacher, administrator, coach, and so on). You can also share this tool with others in the community to obtain their feedback and suggestions. (Refer back to figure 2.2, page 52, for sample responses to an observation and assessment tool.)

# Decision Fatigue Bias Observation and Assessment Tool

**Your Role:** _____

**Type of Bias:** Decision Fatigue Bias _____

**Description of Decision Fatigue Bias:** A cognitive bias that refers to the lack of quality decisions we make after making a lot of decisions or completing repetitious tasks.

| Questions | Answers |
|---|---|
| What do you observe in the classroom or larger school community related to this bias? | |
| What are some possible impacts on students? | |
| What are some possible solutions? | |
| What are the next steps for accomplishing the solution? | |
| What resources or assistance might be needed? | |

## CHAPTER 6

# In-Group Bias

*It's never about belonging to someone; it's about belonging together.*

—Renee Ahdieh

S ociologist William Sumner coined the term *in-group bias* in 1906. He defined in-group bias as "the insiders in a we-group" (Sumner, 1906, p. 12). He further explained that the relationship of those in the "we-group" is often one of "peace, order, law, government, and industry" toward each other. Conversely, he explicates the relationship of "outsiders or others-groups" is often "one of war and plunder" (Sumner, 1906, p. 12). In his book *Folkways*, Sumner (1906) also examines *ethnocentrism*, which is a technical name for the belief that one's own group is the "center of everything" (Sumner, 1906, p. 13). Sumner (1906) continues:

> Each group nourishes its own pride and vanity, boasts itself superior, exalts its own divinities, and looks with contempt on outsiders. Each group thinks its own folkways are the only right ones, and if it observes that other groups have other folkways, these excite its scorn. . . . For our present purpose, the most important fact is that ethnocentrism leads people to exaggerate and intensify everything in their own folkways, which is peculiar, and which differentiates them from others. It, therefore, strengthens its folkways. (p. 58)

Sumner's (1906) explanation of ethnocentrism is the root of in-group bias. A person's *in-group* or *intergroup* can be defined as the social group they are a part of or identify with based on certain characteristics (Sumner, 1906; Tajfel & Turner, 1986). Conversely, an *out-group* or *outergroup* is defined as a social group a person does not

> Often, we develop an affinity for those in our in-group while also developing a bias against those in our out-group.

identify with based on those characteristics they share with their in-group. Often, we develop an affinity for those in our in-group while also developing a bias against those in our out-group. Henri Tajfel and John Turner (1986) write that in-group bias "is a remarkably omnipresent feature of [in-group] relations" (p. 281).

Since Sumner's initial studies, other sociologists have added to the body of work on in-group bias. The research of Marilynn B. Brewer (2007); Logan Hamley, Carla A. Houkamau, Danny Osborne, Fiona Kate Barlow, and Chris G. Sibley (2020); and Tajfel and Turner (1986) also notes the importance of in-groups, while identifying challenges with forming biases toward those who are not in our in-group. Throughout their research, several themes or examples of in-groups emerged.

Figure 6.1 illustrates common categories we typically identify as our in-group. On the outside, there are people scattered around who are not part of that in-group. If you look at your school community, you might see how this illustration shows up in cafeterias, playgrounds, and classrooms. You may also see this show up in who we collaborate and have lunch with. As you study the illustration, think about what aspects you closely identify with. Are you part of the in-group in your school community? Who is in the out-group of your school community and why?

In 2021, author and social psychologist Maykel Verkuyten added to the body of research used to help understand in-group bias. In his article "Group Identity and Ingroup Bias: The Social Identity Approach," Verkuyten (2021) states, "Group identity is simultaneously social and individual, public and private. It is considered a key construct for conceptualizing the relationship between the individual and society" (p. 298).

Naturally, it seems that we have more in common with people in our same ethnic, racial, socioeconomic, religious, or gender groups. For example, whenever I go to conferences, I find myself looking for other African Americans. At times, I feel more comfortable around African American people, regardless of their gender, religious

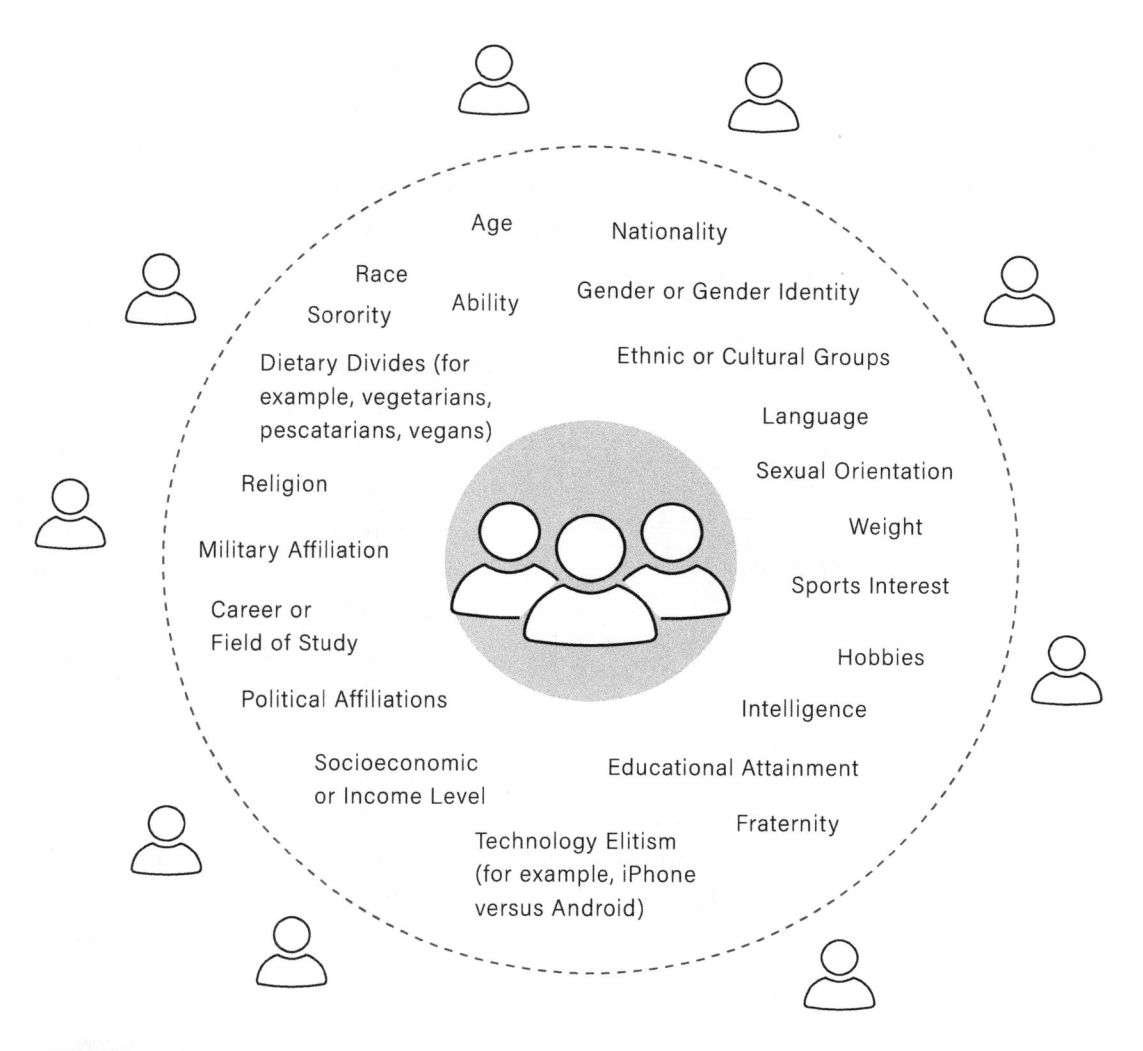

**FIGURE 6.1:** In-group and out-groups.

affiliation, or any other descriptor. While it is often comforting for me to be around other African Americans, I do not discriminate or "other" those who are not part of my racial in-group.

# In-Groups and Othering

Gayatri Spivak coined the term *othering* in 1985 to describe how our views of people often lead to differential treatment. Viewing people who are not in our in-group as inferior can lead to *othering*, treating people differently because they are not part of our social group or in-group (Spivak, 1985). I first experienced othering when my family moved to the suburbs of Chicago during middle school. We were among the few African American students in our school. Outside of the service workers, there were no other people of color working at the school. It was scary, and I often felt intimidated and excluded by my classmates. Not only was I the last to be selected for any cooperative groups, but I also remember being called the "N word" more times than I could count.

> Viewing people who are not in our in-group as inferior can lead to *othering*.

Unfortunately, when I told the teacher and administrator about it, nothing was done. One teacher even told me not to worry about it because the kids were probably just playing. Just "playing" was hurtful. Once I finally fought back, guess who was the only one who got suspended? Me! When my mother, a well-known professional, came to the school to reinstate me, the principal had a police officer in her office. My mother, my champion, expressed her feelings to the principal and police officer without holding anything back. Without cursing or yelling, she let them know that just because we were Black didn't mean we were violent, and the real violent ones weren't suspended like I was. Later, after my mother called the police chief to explain what happened, the officer apologized for his actions. This is just one of the many examples of in-group bias at work in education.

While it is completely natural to gravitate to our in-groups, when we exclude or, worse yet, harm people because they do not belong to these groups, it derails efforts to honor the diversity of school communities.

# Bias Assessment

Use the checklist in figure 6.2 to assess your own in-group bias and check for understanding of this specific cognitive bias. As you reflect on each descriptor, indicate the frequency you relate to each statement. Remember to be honest and give yourself grace. Be gentle with yourself, because in-group bias is often formed when we are children and become consciously aware of our outward appearance and our similarities to and differences from others. This is an opportunity to see yourself more clearly so you can respond in a way that prevents the negative impacts of in-group bias in your school. Following the checklist are two scenarios that will assist in expanding your knowledge of how this bias shows up in schools.

| Descriptor | Most of the Time | Sometimes | Never |
|---|---|---|---|
| During childhood, I had close relationships with children from various ethnic groups other than my own. | | | |
| During childhood, I engaged in family and community events outside of school with people from various ethnic groups other than my own. | | | |
| During childhood, I attended a school with children from different ethnic groups other than my own. | | | |
| During childhood, I socialized with children from different socioeconomic and income levels other than my own. | | | |
| During childhood, I socialized with children from different age groups. | | | |
| As a child, I played with toys that represented different ethnic groups. | | | |
| During childhood, I socialized with children from different age groups other than my own. | | | |
| During childhood, I had friendships with people of opposite genders. | | | |
| During childhood, I had friendships with people with disabilities. | | | |
| As an adult, I have close relationships with people from various ethnic groups. | | | |
| As an adult, I engage in family and community events outside school with people from various ethnic groups. | | | |
| As an adult, I work with people from various ethnic groups. | | | |
| As an adult, I have friendships with people with disabilities. | | | |

**FIGURE 6.2:** In-group bias self-reflection checklist.

continued →

| Descriptor | Most of the Time | Sometimes | Never |
|---|---|---|---|
| As an adult, I socialize with people from different socioeconomic or income levels. | | | |
| As an adult, I have friendships with people who have different sexual identities. | | | |
| As an adult, I have friendships with people of different genders, including cisgender persons of the opposite sex. | | | |
| As an adult, I socialize with people from different age groups other than my own. | | | |
| I attend events that help me learn about different ethnic or cultural groups. | | | |
| I consider the diversity of my school community when making policy decisions. (Only administrators and school board members answer this question.) | | | |
| I consider the diversity of our world by including various ethnic and cultural groups in my reading and other classroom or course materials. | | | |
| I include positive representations of various ethnic and cultural groups in my presentations or other visual aids. | | | |

Reflect on your answers. Consider the following questions to guide your reflections.

1. How do my relationships with people of other races, ethnicities, and genders influence my understanding of diverse cultures?
2. What are some memorable experiences or lessons from these relationships?
3. In what ways do I continue to seek interactions with diverse cultures?
4. What have I learned from my colleagues with different cultural backgrounds?
5. How do I engage and connect with people across various age groups?

*Visit **go.SolutionTree.com/diversityandequity** for a free reproducible version of this figure.*

The interactions or lack thereof that we have as children throughout our development often shape our affinity toward those with whom we share similar attributes. Understanding your upbringing and how you choose to socialize as an adult further solidifies in-group bias. When you understand yourself more clearly, you can better manage your interactions with others both in your in-group and out-group, thus managing in-group bias.

Now that you have taken your personal inventory, read the following scenarios, which illustrate the impact of the in-group bias in schools. After reading each scenario, revisit the checklist to reevaluate your answers.

# Scenario 1

Marjorie was a high school teacher and adviser for the student government association at Prairie High School. This was her twenty-third year of teaching and third year serving as the student activities adviser. She loved assisting and being part of her students' academic and social growth. In addition to her duties at school, she was also a classically trained pianist who played every Sunday in church as well as in the local community orchestra. Working with students gave her opportunities to encourage them to be their best selves. Marjorie was also one of the few teachers who students knew they could go to when they were going through difficulties.

As student activities adviser, she enjoyed helping students create fun events that brought them all together. Some of the popular clubs at Prairie High were the Chorus Club, Drama Club, Latin Club, Students for Atheism, Family Community and Career Leaders of America, Jewish Student Club, Forensics Club, German Club, Gay-Straight Student Alliance, Muslim Students for Change, Spanish Club, STEM Robotics Club, and National Christian Club. She also enjoyed assisting with developing clubs that helped students create a deeper sense of inclusion and belongingness at the school. Marjorie embraced all students, whether they shared her personal beliefs or not, and encouraged them to think outside the box. She would often tell herself that it was wrong to judge and made efforts to be inclusive when making decisions for student organizations.

As adviser, one of Marjorie's roles was to sign off on all financial requests for any activities and equipment. Like her predecessor, she ensured that student organizations had funds for operating costs as well as events by being fiscally responsible and supporting organizations with fundraisers. Unfortunately, it was rumored that she ensured every student organization received funding or activities except for one.

The Gay-Straight Student Alliance (GSSA) was a popular student group. Every year, they shared event ideas that were approved by the former student activities adviser. They noticed that since Marjorie took on that role, they were denied the opportunity of facilitating any events outside their regularly scheduled meetings. When asked about not being approved for their proposed events, Marjorie told them that there wasn't enough money in the budget to cover their event. Students in the GSSA grew even more concerned when they discovered that Marjorie was organizing a beginning-of-the-year student club showcase, which all organizations were asked to be part of . . . well, all except GSSA. GSSA members decided to submit a letter to the administrators. Janice, a member of GSSA, received advice from her parents who were both lawyers. The parents of GSSA arranged a meeting with Marjorie and the school principal to address this concern.

During the meeting, Marjorie repeatedly shared that she supported all student organizations fairly. However, when presented with the facts that not only was GSSA not given funding for events but also left out of the showcase, Marjorie became defensive and said, "They are not the same as the other students." She explained to the principal and parents that she was OK with "them" having a student organization but was very concerned about "them" having events that would "taint the rest of the student body." Parents were appalled and grateful they decided earlier not to include students at the meeting.

The principal asked if she could speak with Marjorie alone, but before they left, the parents demanded that she be fired. They explained that her blatant discrimination and inequitable treatment of students was based on her views toward their sexual orientation. After the parents left, the principal asked Marjorie to step down as the student activities adviser. The principal, a friend who also attended the same gym as Marjorie, did not want her to lose her job, so she recommended that she attend cultural awareness training. The principal understood that being an educator meant supporting all students and wanted Marjorie to learn more about the LGBTQ+ community and other diverse populations.

Marjorie learned a lot during the diversity, equity, and inclusion training. She used the strategies she learned to become an even better teacher. Additionally, after learning about the ways many LGBTQ+ youth were ostracized by their families and community, she became an ally and chose to extend her learning by completing safe space training. She also apologized to GSSA members and their families.

# Scenario 2

Jade Middle School was in a prominent area of Virginia. Due to the presence of various military bases in this area, including the U.S. Navy, Air Force, and Army, there were many people from various ethnic and religious backgrounds. In the neighborhood zoned for Jade Middle School, there were families from Greece, France, Belgium, Turkey, Canada, and Albania. There was also a good mix of families from Virginia and other parts of the United States. There was a synagogue, mosque, Catholic church, and Buddhist temple all within a five-mile radius of this community.

In the past five years, a growing population of Muslim students attended Jade Middle School. Administrators and teachers worked together to determine how to best serve this diverse student body. During certain diversity months, they hung posters around the school and encouraged students to read books based on the diversity focus of the month. Additionally, the cafeteria offered a special menu during diversity months like Asian and Pacific Islander Heritage Month, Hispanic Heritage Month, Black History Month, and others. Their goal was to make sure they honored the diversity of their student body. Unfortunately, they did not ask parents or students to assist them with strategies and tips to honor these various cultures.

On the day of Yom Kippur, one of the most sacred Jewish holy days, mathematics teacher Mr. Glass scheduled a huge pop quiz. One of the ways the Jewish community honors Yom Kippur is by having a full day of rest, which includes fasting, no work, and no driving. Five students, who were all Jewish, were absent and missed the quiz. When they returned to school the next day as Mr. Glass began to pass out the graded pop quizzes, they asked about how to make up the missing pop quiz. He asked why they were absent. None of the students felt comfortable explaining why they were absent in front of their classmates, so they didn't say anything.

Later, when they got home from school, the students discussed the situation with their families, and they collectively decided to email Mr. Glass. When he explained that not only was he not going to give students an opportunity to make up the quiz, but the pop quiz would also be counted against them since there was no explanation for their absence, families requested a meeting with the school principal. During the meeting, parents shared with Mr. Glass and the principal the importance of Yom Kippur and asked that their children be allowed to do some type of project or another quiz to make up for this missing grade.

Mr. Glass was apologetic after listening to the parents and learning about the significance of this sacred day to their community. He gladly offered to give a makeup quiz to the students. Additionally, the principal, in collaboration with Mr. Glass and other teachers, decided to form a parent advisory group to help them understand how to best serve the diverse needs of the student population and other ways to bridge the school-to-community gap. Through the work of the parent advisory group, they learned about other holy days associated with the Jewish, Buddhist, Muslim, and other religious faiths. Teachers decided to not have tests and quizzes on those days.

---

Making decisions can be difficult at times. Making decisions that involve people who belong to our in-group when it involves someone from our out-group can be even more difficult. In the previous scenarios, Marjorie and Mr. Glass were involved in situations that involved in-group bias. Although Marjorie considered herself an ally for diversity and inclusion, her personal view of students in the GSSA caused her to deny them funding. She also did not include them in the student club showcase event out of fear that they would somehow taint other students. Her comments were not only insensitive and hurtful; they were also biased. Had she had a better understanding of same-gender-loving students and those who form alliances with them, maybe she would have handled herself differently.

Mr. Glass was an educator who simply didn't know what he didn't know. The Jewish community was not part of his in-group; therefore, their holy days weren't on his radar or considered when scheduling pop quizzes. His initial decision to have the pop quiz and not allow the five students to make it up was based on in-group bias associated with religion. Although it was not his intention to harm students by denying them the opportunity to take another quiz, Mr. Glass's initial decision to do so caused harm. Fortunately, after learning about Yom Kippur and other religious holy days people in their diverse school community honor, he, along with other teachers, were able to make truly inclusive decisions. Because of Mr. Glass's willingness to learn about a religion in his out-group, he was able to be part of a win-win decision for them all.

## PAUSE AND PONDER

- How did the two educators and school community demonstrate in-group bias?

- Recall a time when a decision was made in your favor because of your affiliation with a certain group. How did you benefit from this favoritism or in-group bias? Did this decision cause harm to others outside your in-group? How did you feel knowing that a decision was made because of the affinity of your in-group over another? Were you angry, sad, hurt, or unsettled?

- Now, let's focus on students. Think back to a time when you made a decision that favored a student from your in-group that involved another student from your out-group. Was your initial reaction to side in favor of the in-group student? What didn't you consider? How do you think the student in your in-group felt when your decision was in their favor? How do you think your decision impacted the student in your out-group?

As educators, we are faced with decisions involving people from our in-group and out-group. We will not always know the exact right thing to say or do; however, when we make decisions or fail to make decisions because of our own biases or lack of understanding regarding people in our out-group, it creates dysfunction in school communities.

## PAUSE AND PONDER

Think back to your experiences making decisions about students in your in-groups and out-groups. How did your affinity for someone in your in-group impact your decision? How would it have made you feel to know that the decision

continued →

makers made efforts to learn about you before making a decision that negatively impacted you? Would you have felt grateful they put themselves in your shoes? How could there have been a win-win?

In the previous scenarios, someone was impacted by another person's lack of understanding, knowledge, and compassion toward an out-group. Marjorie's personal beliefs regarding the LGBTQ+ community, especially same-gender-loving men and women, were harmful to students. Mr. Glass lacked knowledge of the Jewish community and the importance of Yom Kippur. They were not part of his in-group, therefore, they weren't considered.

## Tips for Counteracting In-Group Bias

As previously noted, counteracting any bias begins with taking a breath. When the subconscious mind is at work, we need to take an intentional step back, beginning with a deep breath. The following are some suggestions for counteracting in-group bias.

- Take an intentional deep breath.
- Acknowledge that it is OK to have affinity toward those with whom you share ethnic, language, gender, socioeconomic, and other commonalities. Being honest with yourself helps you to extend yourself grace, which may assist you in extending the same to those you don't readily share commonalities with.

> Make a point to learn about other cultures, ethnic groups, languages, religions, and so on.

- Make a point to learn about other cultures, ethnic groups, languages, religions, and so on, as expanding your awareness of others may help you see it is possible to share commonalities with people who present differently. I use the term *present differently* to describe the outward appearance of someone who may be different from my outward appearance. As human beings, we are so much more than our outward appearance. Learning about cultures outside of your own may help you to see you have a lot more in common with others than you think.

- Visualize the person you are making decisions about as *you*, then ask yourself, "How would I like to be treated?"

- Understand your decision impacts another person, not an idea or stereotype, but someone who also needs to be seen, valued, and heard.

- Interact and spend time with others outside of your in-group.

- Ask for advice or guidance from others. Make an intentional effort to include those from diverse backgrounds.

- Encourage and plan intentional opportunities for diverse groups to work together through cooperative learning projects.

- Avoid complaining to others about situations that involve those outside of your in-group. Sometimes, when we complain to others in our in-group about people from our out-group, it can deepen our bias because it solidifies an "us versus them" mentality and can lead to tension, resentment, and unfair decision making.

- Establish merit-based performance reviews that clearly outline how educators are evaluated. This helps mitigate in-group bias when reviewing people in your in-group and protects those in your out-group from being evaluated unfairly.

- Create and use grading rubrics to assess assignments. Like merit-based performance reviews, this can help curb issues with in-group bias.

- Stick to the facts of a situation and listen to how students and others in your educational community feel. Being aware of how our decisions impact others can help stimulate empathy.

- Honor the diversity within your educational communities by seeing and celebrating differences. This helps ensure that

> Honor the diversity within your educational communities by seeing and celebrating differences.

people don't feel they have to assimilate to be included and that we include people from our out-group, thus expanding our capacity to make non-in-group-bias decisions.

- Avoid siding with someone just because you identify more closely with them as part of your own in-group.

- Avoid vilifying someone because they aren't part of your in-group.

- Postpone decisions if you feel you have to defend or come to the rescue of someone from your in-group. While feeling protective of someone in your social group or in-group may be natural, making decisions to protect them from a fellow educator who is not in your social group or in-group without understanding the facts can be detrimental.

In-group bias can be one of the easiest biases to develop. Like many of us, as a child, I associated safety, security, and family with those who looked like me. Admittedly, there is a certain comfort I feel around other African American cisgender women from the south side of Chicago. I went to a predominantly Black school and a predominantly Black church. When my family relocated to a predominantly White community that was not too kind to me, I stayed close to the other African American students. The desire to be around other African Americans is not wrong. Similarly, the desire for European or White, Japanese, Latinx/Hispanic, Native American, Cambodian, Haitian, Hawaiian, Bosnian, or other ethnic groups to live and feel comfortable around each other is not wrong, either.

> Being aware of and utilizing strategies to mitigate our tendency to favor our in-groups is a huge factor in cultivating equitable and inclusive school communities.

We all have in-groups we feel more connected to than others. However, when feelings of belonging cause us to place value judgments on those in out-groups, it can lead to in-group bias. This bias can taint our perceptions of those to whom we relate more closely and those we don't. Tainted perceptions, whether conscious or unconscious, lead to flawed decisions that create inequities and hurt. While we may not be able to erase our desire to be around those with whom we share commonalities, as humans and educators, we are responsible for the decisions we make that impact students. Being aware of and utilizing strategies to mitigate our tendency to favor our in-groups is a huge factor in cultivating equitable and inclusive school communities.

## Next Steps

The "In-Group Bias Observation and Assessment Tool" (page 118) can help you observe and assess incidences of in-group bias happening in the classroom or larger school community and plan next steps. You can use this tool regardless of your role in the school (teacher, administrator, coach, and so on). You can also share this tool with others in the community to obtain their feedback and suggestions. (Refer back to figure 2.2, page 52, for sample responses to an observation and assessment tool.)

# In-Group Bias Observation and Assessment Tool

**Your Role:** _____

**Type of Bias:** In-Group Bias _____

**Description of In-Group Bias:** A cognitive bias that explains our tendency to favor and make decisions that support those with whom we share the same in-group or share physical, cultural, religious, language, and other similarities.

| Questions | Answers |
|---|---|
| What do you observe in the classroom or larger school community related to this bias? | |
| What are some possible impacts on students? | |
| What are some possible solutions? | |
| What are the next steps for accomplishing the solution? | |
| What resources or assistance might be needed? | |

## CHAPTER 7

# Scarcity Bias

*Fear is the path to the dark side. Fear leads to
anger. Anger leads to hate. Hate leads to suffering.*

—Yoda

Scarcity bias is a cognitive shortcut rooted in the fear of lack. In 1975, Stephen Worchel, a psychologist at the University of Virginia, first coined the term *scarcity bias* (Worchel, Lee, & Adewole, 1975). During research conducted with Worchel, Jerry Lee and Akanbi Adewole gathered 134 participants and put them into two equal groups. Both groups were given a cookie from identical jars. Participants in one group selected a cookie from an almost empty jar, while the second group selected theirs from a full jar. Participants of this study were asked to judge the quality, appeal, and monetary value of each cookie. Interestingly, participants who selected cookies from the almost empty jar indicated they were willing to pay 25 percent more than those who selected cookies from the fuller jar.

This foundational study led to the conclusion that "as human beings we tend to place a higher value on things that we see as scarce. Additionally, the more difficult it is to acquire an item, the more value an item has" (Worchel et al., 1975, p. 908). Worchel, Lee, and Adewole's (1975) research led to many other studies that came to similar conclusions. In 2017, Wi-Suk Kwon, Gopikrishna Deshpande, and Jeffrey Katz from Auburn University, along with Sang-Eun Byun, professor of neuroscience from the University of South Carolina, conducted a study and concluded the following about scarcity bias.

> Scarcity may shift the reference point regarding available decision making . . .
> the sense of urgency hinders decision makers' ability to analytically process
> cost and benefits in a balanced manner, driving their cognitive resources to
> be focused on processing benefits (i.e., symbolic values), while suppressing
> resources to process other thoughts . . . findings of this study are relevant
> across a broad range of contexts because choices involving scarcity under-
> lie many of society's most pressing decisions. (Kwon, Deshpande, Katz, &
> Byun, 2017, p. 2)

Robert Cialdini, professor emeritus of psychology and marketing at Arizona State University, performed additional research on scarcity in the book *Influence: The Psychology of Persuasion* (2007). Cialdini (2007) identifies scarcity as one of the principles of persuasion in marketing and sales. He summarizes scarcity as the "perception of dwindling supply of a limited and valuable product" (p. 15). He highlighted two main reasons that scarcity influences our behavior.

1. Because we are hardwired to resist losing freedom of choice, scarcity limits the availability of all the opportunities available to us, especially in complex or complicated situations.

2. Our brains create alternative pathways or shortcuts that help us navigate through complex or complicated situations, therefore seeking the path of least resistance.

> Scarcity bias
> can be one of the
> most invasive
> and uncomfortable
> biases.

Scarcity bias can be one of the most invasive and uncomfortable biases. The feeling of rushing through decisions, not having enough time and energy, is hard. Like many, when I feel I do not have enough time, energy, or money, there is an uncomfortable tightness in my body that affects my mood, decision making, and quality of life. Being stressed while making decisions that impact others, especially students, can cause us to make rushed decisions that may or may not be the best. Conversely, honoring and managing time while also being intentional about allowing ourselves the space we need to make well-informed decisions is one of the greatest services we can offer ourselves and our school communities.

When we feel like we are working nonstop, the brain wants to take cognitive shortcuts. Scarcity bias is a cognitive shortcut that can impact many aspects of our lives, both professional and personal. Being afraid that there is a limited quantity of something we really want may drive us to purchase it even if it's overpriced. Similarly, being afraid that we may not have enough time to get to know students because we have so much to teach can drive us to make general plans for students which may only meet the needs of some students instead of all. Being afraid we don't have enough money to afford the supplemental materials for students can lead us to utilize the resources we already have, even when they're outdated.

Being afraid there are not enough substitute teachers to cover classrooms so educators can go to professional development leads administrators to spending those funds on something else, which directly impacts a teacher's ability to stay abreast of research-based practices that empower them to be better educators. Being afraid we do not have enough time to eat leads us to skip meals, which may impact our health and our cognitive ability to make good decisions for ourselves and our students. Being afraid we don't have enough time to rest because we think productivity means planning for every minute and every second without allowing ourselves proper rest and relaxation may negatively impact our cognitive abilities and interfere with how we make decisions for ourselves as well as for our school community.

When scarcity plays a role in decision making, people tend to cling to the easiest path or the one that provides the most control. This might cause us to make different choices than we would under normal circumstances.

# Scarcity and Decision Making

When we operate out of fear of scarcity, that same fear of loss can influence our decisions. Meng Zhu, professor of business at John Hopkins University, and Rebecca Ratner, professor of marketing at the University of Maryland, also examined the impact of scarcity on our choices and decisions (Zhu & Ratner, 2015). They conducted five experiments that concluded that the overall perception of scarcity induces

> When we operate out of fear or scarcity, that same fear of loss can influence our decisions.

arousal, which can polarize our decisions. Additionally, they detailed the following four stages of decision making through a scarcity mindset.

- **Stage 1: Information processing and initial consideration of alternatives**—This stage involves gathering initial information and learning about the variety of possibilities related to those choices or alternatives.

- **Stage 2: Evaluation of alternatives**—At this stage, Zhu and Ratner (2015) discuss the effects of scarcity as we evaluate alternatives.

- **Stage 3: Choice**—In this stage, we examine the effects of our choices amid feeling scarcity.

- **Stage 4: Consumption experiences**—In this stage, we deal with the effects of making decisions based on scarcity and their impact on our experiences, as well as how our decisions impact others.

> The fear of scarcity or not having enough can immobilize our ability to make well-informed decisions, thus causing decision paralysis.

The fear of scarcity or not having enough can immobilize our ability to make well-informed decisions, thus causing decision paralysis. *Decision paralysis* is a term used to describe the difficulty or our inability to make decisions out of fear (Ansoff, 1957). As human beings, we are motivated by numerous factors, including fear. When we are afraid of losing something of great value, such as time, money, and other resources, decision paralysis can detour us and the school communities we serve.

Although most research on scarcity bias focuses on finances and sales, much of it is applicable to education. In my twenty-six years as an educator, I have had the pleasure of working in various capacities. During my work as a classroom teacher, I was often concerned about having enough time to facilitate lessons in meaningful ways that would help students fully grasp and apply new concepts. I felt that going from one lesson to the next in a timely yet in-depth way for my neurodiverse students was exceedingly difficult. I was not alone.

When I became a statewide literacy trainer, I learned that a lot of educators, including classroom teachers and administrators, shared similar concerns about scarcity of time. There seemed to be, and probably still is, a general concern that, as educators, we don't have enough time to teach the wide variety of lessons we are responsible for while dealing with behavioral concerns, parents, teaching character development, and the infamous "other duties as assigned."

Now, as an administrator, I still often have concerns about there being enough time to accomplish the various tasks I need to do to perform my job with fidelity. Coupled with concerns about scarcity of time, as many other administrators are familiar with, scarcity of financial resources to take care of the expenses associated with being efficient in my role is also often a concern. I am fortunate to be part of several professional groups in which concerns about scarcity of time and finances, including work-life balance, are often topics of discussion when focusing on school improvement and meeting the diverse needs of school communities.

> Although most research on scarcity bias focuses on finances and sales, much of it is applicable to education.

Although the original research on scarcity bias focused on sales, consumerism, and marketing, much of the research relates to how educators make decisions out of fear of not having enough.

## Bias Assessment

Use the checklist in figure 7.1 (page 124) to assess your own scarcity bias and check for understanding of this specific cognitive bias. As you reflect on each descriptor, indicate the frequency you relate to each statement. Again, remember to be honest and give yourself grace. This is an opportunity to see yourself more clearly so you can respond differently in situations and circumstances when scarcity of time, money, and other resources motivate your decisions. Following the checklist are two scenarios that will assist in expanding your knowledge of how this bias shows up in schools.

| Descriptor | Most of the Time | Sometimes | Never |
|---|---|---|---|
| I feel I have enough time to be effective in my role in my school community. | | | |
| I feel I have enough time to plan lessons and activities that highlight a diverse population of people, including, but not limited to, students with disabilities (physical, emotional, neurological, seen and unseen), various races, ethnicities, genders, religions, and so on. | | | |
| I feel my school community prioritizes investing in professional development to assist me in being effective in my role. | | | |
| I feel I have enough material and supplies to be effective in my role. | | | |
| I feel I have a healthy work-life balance. | | | |
| I feel I have enough time to plan and prepare lessons and learning activities to ensure the success of my students. | | | |
| I feel I am afforded the time needed to attend professional development. | | | |
| I feel I am afforded the financial resources needed to attend professional development. | | | |
| I feel I have enough time to meet the diverse needs of my students. (Only teachers answer this question.) | | | |
| I feel I have enough time to help meet the diverse needs of teachers in my school community. (Only administrators answer this question.) | | | |
| I feel frustrated about the limited time I have to be effective in my role in my school community. | | | |
| I feel fatigued or emotionally drained while working to accomplish duties to be effective in my role in my school community. | | | |
| I tend to intentionally gather all the facts before making decisions, including listening to other perspectives, even when it may take additional time to do so. | | | |

| I feel pressured by time when making decisions as an educator. | | | |
|---|---|---|---|
| I trust there is enough money to purchase resources (material, programs, supplies, and so on) needed to effectively meet the needs of my students. | | | |
| I trust there are enough financial resources to build and maintain effective school programs and classes to meet the diverse needs of my school community. | | | |

Reflect on your answers. Consider the following questions to guide your reflections.

1. How do I currently manage my time, energy, and resources to be effective?

2. What changes or support could help me better manage my time, energy, and resources?

3. How do I currently manage my work-life balance?

4. How do I allocate time for planning and preparation for the diverse needs of my students?

5. What additional professional development might I need to be more effective in my role?

**FIGURE 7.1:** Scarcity bias self-reflection checklist.

*Visit **go.SolutionTree.com/diversityandequity** for a free reproducible version of this figure.*

Now that you have taken your personal inventory, read the following scenarios, which illustrate the impact of scarcity bias in schools. After reading each scenario, revisit the checklist to reevaluate your answers.

# Scenario 1

Greenleaf School District is home to one high school, two middle schools, and three elementary schools. This school district is situated in a rural area known for gang violence, dilapidated housing, teenage pregnancy, and elevated high school dropout rates. Most of the students coming from middle school were ill-prepared for the level of academic rigor required to be successful in high school. Middle school teachers blamed the elementary schools for students' not having the proper foundation in literacy to allow them to succeed academically at the middle school. Similarly, for a long time, high school teachers were vocal about complaints that elementary and middle school teachers were sending them students who read below grade level and struggled mathematically.

The district's slogan, "Achieving Excellence Together," was not a practical reality for many students, teachers, parents, or administrators. For example, for two years, one of the elementary schools utilized funds to acquire extensive professional development focused on literacy. The consultants commissioned to support teachers provided research-based, job-embedded, and ongoing training that included both whole- and small-group instruction. The two elementary schools that participated in literacy training with these consultants were required to make a three-year commitment to allow teachers and students to acclimate to new literacy instruction.

Due to fear and concerns about availability of substitute teachers, school administrators at the elementary schools did not allow teachers to attend professional development. Instead, they worked with outside literacy consultants to ensure the professional development teachers received was job embedded. Additionally, teachers met with literacy consultants two to three times per week during planning time and after school until 4:30 p.m. Literacy consultants also came into classrooms to model strategies. They visited classrooms throughout the day to observe and support teachers with utilizing new strategies during whole- and small-group instruction. Consequently, those two elementary schools have seen a spike in their reading comprehension scores. The two schools have also received honorable mention in the local newspaper and have been a topic of discussion at the local board meeting, especially because mathematics scores also improved.

The ability to comprehend complex word problems is in part due to a student's ability to understand complex text. Although teachers and students were celebrated at both elementary schools, the excitement was not shared by everyone in the district, especially the elementary school that was not receiving professional development. The middle schools also became interested in receiving training, as teachers were struggling to differentiate learning for students who were significantly below grade level.

During one of the administrators' meetings, three principals expressed concerns about the inequities in professional development impacting students in literacy. The superintendent reminded them they all were given the same amount of professional development funds and encouraged them to rethink how they were utilizing them. During that meeting, two things became clear: (1) administrators were not allowing teachers to attend any external professional development, and (2) administrators also were too afraid to allow the job-embedded professional development, fearing teachers would not have enough time. They were using their professional development funds to invest in webinars teachers could access at their leisure. Because they were afraid teachers would not commit to staying after school for professional development, they thought webinars were a good alternative.

This led to a conversation with the director of the literacy agency, who encouraged the administrators to reinvest their funds to offer teachers a stipend to attend after-school professional development. Since the webinars were not very costly, they had enough funds in their professional development budgets to award teachers a stipend to stay after school and pay for literacy training. By slowing down to examine the situation more carefully, they were able to explore ways to institute the same type of literacy professional development that was helping the other schools improve. Instead of allowing their fear of teachers not having time to attend professional development to get in the way of much-needed training to enhance literacy instruction for students, they implemented a stipend for teachers to attend after-school professional development. To their surprise, 100 percent of the teachers stayed after school twice a week for training!

Fortunately, the literacy agency had the capacity to service the entire district. Within five years, the high school, as well as all the other schools in the district, received the Blue Ribbon Award, recognition by the U.S. Department of Education for academic excellence.

# Scenario 2

Mrs. Rose was a new third-grade teacher at Seaside Elementary School. She enjoyed teaching and getting to know her students' interests. Third grade was a pivotal year for students, as this was the first time they would take the state standardized test. Encouraging students' interest in both fiction and nonfiction reading was crucial to their success. Mrs. Rose knew students would be expected to not only answer multiple-choice questions based on fiction and nonfiction text, but they would also be expected to answer open-ended questions to demonstrate their depth-of-reading comprehension.

As a new teacher, Mrs. Rose really wanted to stimulate and expand her students' love of reading. She wanted to make sure students were exposed to a wide variety of text, including books that were of interest to her diverse group of students, most of whom were African American and Hispanic boys. The former third-grade teacher had gifted Mrs. Rose with two bookshelves of nonfiction and fiction books that could be used for small-group instruction, read alouds, or independent reading times. Students also had access to the school library, which they could utilize during their scheduled time once a week.

After giving students a reading interest survey to assess the types of topics they were interested in, Mrs. Rose quickly noticed there were not enough books that included topics most of the boys in her class enjoyed. She spoke with the librarian but did not get the support for which she'd hoped. The librarian made it clear that over the past few years, many other teachers had also requested books, including topics that interested boys. Mrs. Rose was told that due to budget constraints, the library had not received new books for quite some time. She wanted to know how much money the library was awarded every year for the purchase of new books. After asking the librarian more questions about the allocation of funds for books, she discovered the librarian had no clue about the budget! Evidently, the librarian assumed there were no funds and had been too afraid to ask.

Feeling frustrated, Mrs. Rose decided she would focus her efforts on expanding her classroom library as opposed to the whole school library. She reached out to some of her colleagues and other educator friends at different schools to seek advice about how to expand her in-class library. She learned a lack of clarity about financial resources to purchase quality and relevant teaching materials was a common issue facing a lot of elementary and middle school teachers. Additionally, there was also a concern among her peers that there were not enough funds to purchase books from year to year. Some libraries at other schools also did not carry up-to-date books that appealed to a wide variety of interests, especially those of boys. A friend who worked at another school told her about a list of grants especially designated for libraries and classroom teachers. These grant funds helped schools create more robust reading selections for students by affording teachers and librarians the money to purchase books.

At first, Mrs. Rose looked at the grant application and decided she did not have enough time to submit the required information. She allowed another school semester to go by without revisiting the need for additional books. Between her personal life and classroom duties, she felt a scarcity of time already, so she didn't apply for the grant. That summer, Mrs. Rose decided to take action and revisit the grant application. To her amazement, it was a fairly simple application that only took about an hour to complete. About a month later, right before the start of another school year, she was approved for two grants totaling $1,500.

For a while, Mrs. Rose felt bad about not investing the time to apply for the grant sooner. She realized her fear of not having enough time to commit to completing the application got the best of her. So, she utilized the grant funds to order books for her classroom and shared the list of grants with the school librarian, along with her other colleagues. After overhearing some of the students from Mrs. Rose's class talking about the exciting new books they were reading, the librarian decided to take the time to complete the grant. It had been a long time since the librarian heard students this excited about reading. She decided the time and effort involved in submitting grant applications was worth the impact it would have on all students in the elementary school who visited the library. The librarian decided to submit an application to completely update the books in the school library for students in grades K–8.

With Mrs. Rose's help, it took the librarian about three to four hours to complete several grant applications. Within a month, the librarian received email correspondence indicating that the library at Seaside Elementary School was being awarded a $4,000 grant. She utilized grant funds to expand the variety of nonfiction and fiction texts. The librarian also took things a step further and conducted an interest inventory for all elementary students to ensure she purchased books on a wide variety of topics they would be interested in for years to come. Overcoming the fear of not having enough time to submit the grant to upgrade the school library was worth the effort and did not take as much time as she had feared.

---

We all have felt pressed for time. Some of us may feel like we never have enough time. This feeling of scarcity, whether it is with time or money, can lead us to postpone important decisions or rush through them. As educators, we often must facilitate lessons for students on various academic levels. Additionally, we have a set amount of content or skills to teach students so they may successfully go on to the next skill or grade level. Educators are also human beings with families and additional responsibilities and hobbies outside the school community.

## PAUSE AND PONDER

- How did the two scenarios demonstrate the cognitive bias known as scarcity bias?

- Recall a time when a decision was made in a hurry due to scarcity of time. Additionally, recall a time when a decision was postponed or nullified due to scarcity of financial resources. How did this decision impact you or others in your school community? How did you feel knowing a decision was made in haste or due to perceived scarcity of resources? Did you feel rushed? If a decision rushed because of scarcity of time, did you feel unsettled or frustrated?

- Now, let's focus on students. Recall a time when you made a hurried decision that impacted students. Maybe it was toward the end of the school day, and you rushed through learning material. You could have been pressed for time, ready to go home, or pressured to move on to other concepts to cover. When there is scarcity of time, we may be tempted to take shortcuts and rush decisions without considering all the facts. We may also neglect covering learning materials thoroughly because we feel rushed. In these situations, we may be more susceptible to making decisions due to scarcity bias. Does this sound familiar?

- Recognize a time you or someone in your school community made a decision based on a lack of resources that impacted students. How did you know that a different decision could have been made? Were there other financial resources that could have been considered? Could you or the person making the decision have made the decision later, when scarcity of time was not an issue? How do you think your decisions made your students feel? How did the decision impact your students and the school community at large?

Administrators and others who are responsible for financial decisions that impact the school community may often feel like there is not enough money or enough time to do everything they need to do. The wide variety of materials and other resources students need to thrive, in addition to costly professional development educators need to efficiently educate students, can be overwhelming. When we are scared or afraid of not having enough time, energy, or money to meet our own needs, let alone the needs of the school community, it can be easy to make decisions rooted in scarcity bias. The following is a list of tips you can use to proactively avoid or navigate through scarcity bias.

# Tips for Counteracting Scarcity Bias

Again, counteracting any bias begins with taking a breath. Breathing deeply allows us to relax and open our minds to think more clearly. We can take an intentional step back to reflect. The following are some suggestions for counteracting the scarcity bias.

- Take an intentional deep breath. Centering aids the brain in slowing down, which balances the adrenaline levels that can prompt us to make rushed decisions.
- Allow yourself and any other administrators or educators time to gather information before making a decision. This tip is especially important when making a discipline decision about a student who may have had challenges in the past.
- Pause to recognize all possibilities before making financial, professional development, student, or personnel decisions.
- Save cognitive resources by breaking up large projects into smaller chunks.
- Reduce the sense of urgency that occurs when an immediate decision needs to be made by concentrating efforts on one (or two at most) tasks.
- Resist the urge to multitask.
- Limit distractions such as social media and other time fillers used as avoidance behaviors.
- Get proper rest. Yes, that means seven to nine hours of sleep per night.
- Allow yourself break time or a daytime nap. Education is a big job! It requires a lot of time, energy, and cognitive presence. Giving yourself time to rest increases productivity and the brain's capacity to focus.
- Be honest with yourself so you can also be honest with others when you feel pressured for time.
- Manage your time wisely. This can help avoid that feeling of working nonstop.

Following the strategies outlined in this chapter can help counteract or manage scarcity bias. As with the story of the tortoise and the hare, sometimes it's important to remember that moving fast does not always equate to moving efficiently. Sometimes, especially when our decisions can have long-term impacts on students and the school community, slow and steady may be the key that helps us win the race for more inclusive school communities where all students are seen, valued, heard, and empowered with educational skills that benefit our communities and the world.

## Next Steps

The "Scarcity Bias Observation and Assessment Tool" (page 134) can help you observe and assess incidences of scarcity bias happening in the classroom or larger school community and plan next steps. You can use this tool regardless of your role in the school (teacher, administrator, coach, and so on). You can also share this tool with others in the community to obtain their feedback and suggestions. (Refer back to figure 2.2, page 52, for sample responses to an observation and assessment tool.)

# Scarcity Bias Observation and Assessment Tool

**Your Role:** _____

**Type of Bias:** Scarcity Bias _____

**Description of Scarcity Bias:** A heuristic or mental shortcut that occurs when we fear the loss of something valuable, such as time, energy, or money that biases or colors our decisions.

| Questions | Answers |
|---|---|
| What do you observe in the classroom or larger school community related to this bias? | |
| What are some possible impacts on students? | |
| What are some possible solutions? | |
| What are the next steps for accomplishing the solution? | |
| What resources or assistance might be needed? | |

# Epilogue

One Saturday night in 1982, Eddie Murphy and Louis Gossett Jr. were on air performing a *Saturday Night Live* skit. The skit portrayed a toxic relationship between an African American father and son. It also portrayed some stereotypes about the African American community, such as alcoholism, poor education, single-parent households, and poverty. In the middle of the skit, the character played by Eddie Murphy looked at Louis Gossett Jr. and said, "What are we doing? This seems biased." He asked for the writers and questioned why they wrote a skit portraying African Americans in such a bad light. He also wanted to know why Gossett was being portrayed as a bad father.

Gossett and Murphy then went on to correct some of the myths and stereotypes included in the skit. They made it clear that not every African American household was poor, and that many were wealthy, lived in two-parent households, and excelled academically (Saturday Night Live, 1982). These myths portrayed on national television are rooted in bias. Just as Louis Gossett Jr. and Eddie Murphy corrected these biases, we too must do the work to manage and eliminate the biases that often plague our school communities. It wasn't until 2016, when I attended a professional development workshop on culturally responsive teaching and learning with Sharroky Hollie, that it occurred to me—underneath all our attempts to improve school communities, there may be a lot of unchecked biases inadvertently sabotaging our efforts (S. Hollie, personal communication, September 15, 2019).

> Underneath all
> our attempts to
> improve school
> communities, there
> may be a lot of
> unchecked biases
> inadvertently
> sabotaging
> our efforts.

As a classroom teacher, I was privileged to have principals and instructional coaches who provided ongoing professional development. I worked in an inner-city school where we had professional development to assist us with implementing best practices in improving literacy and reading comprehension skills, utilizing manipulatives in mathematics, classroom management, depth of knowledge (DOK), and so much more. Although all the teachers in the school had a similar demographic of students from the same neighborhood, we repeatedly observed major differences in students' academic growth, even those in the same grade.

One of the key differences was the classroom teacher's mindset about students. For example, some teachers who took part in professional development would comment aloud that "our students can't learn this." Others would murmur the same sentiment and go back to their classrooms and change nothing.

I remember one time our school principal started to intentionally make rounds with the expectation of seeing us implement new strategies we had been learning. She was infuriated. Although teachers had the strategies, biases were blocking implementing them in ways that could help their students soar. I have witnessed educators leave a vital member of their instructional community out of important conversations because of bias. I have even been asked to resign from a teaching position at a university because of bias (I will share that story in my next book or workshop).

This book contains examples and occurrences of biases that I have been a part of and witnessed firsthand. In the words of one of my elders, Sauda Smith, "This ain't for play play!" (S. Smith, personal communication, October 2, 2023). Learning about our biases and utilizing strategies to correct them before doing harm is not for play. The intentional cultivation of school communities that are equitable and inclusive are not for play. Enjoying school communities where everyone is seen and valued in meaningful ways and that encourage learning and accelerated academic achievement is not for play. Cultivating systemic equitable and inclusive learning is not for play. Fostering school communities that are psychologically and physiologically safe is not for play.

It is my belief that no amount of professional development geared toward academic or other forms of school improvement will work unless we also have a better understanding of our biases so we can mitigate any negative impact our biases may cause. If you are unsure of the impact of biases on your school community, I encourage you to conduct a climate and culture survey. This will help you gain insight on your school communities' perceptions regarding the effectiveness of current practices geared toward fostering a sense of belonging, which is a precursor to academic achievement. If your school engages in a climate and culture survey, I implore you to honor the shared insights by creating an action plan to improve any policies or practices that may be negatively impacting your school community. Additionally, implementing an anonymous bias reporting system where students and educators can report incidents of bias they witness, or have been a part of, without fear of retaliation is another proactive way to learn more about the ways biases are impacting your school community.

Educational spaces are supposed to be safe from harm. However, the reality is that we all are biased. Accept that. Being biased does not make us bad people. It does not make us wrong or guilty and does not need to be coupled with shame. Not learning about our biases and not being proactive about managing or using strategies to minimize the impact of our biases is the problem, not the bias itself. School communities that are inclusive, equitable, and intentionally cultivate belongingness are educated about their biases and proactively do something about them. That journey begins with us. In the words of late Grandmother Hoover C. Kizart, "When you know better, you do better."

This book provides the knowledge and information you need to start addressing and eliminating bias in your school. Now, what will you do? Remember, biases take time to develop; some are hardwired in our subconscious minds. These will be the

> School communities that are inclusive, equitable, and intentionally cultivate belongingness are educated about their biases and proactively do something about them.

trickiest ones to manage or eliminate. Be observant of yourself first. Do your best to reflect on your thoughts, practices, policies, curriculum, lessons, and relationships with colleagues and stakeholders. As you reflect, give yourself grace, and make a change. Our future leaders depend on us to help cultivate a better world.

# References and Resources

Achieve.org. (2018). *On track or falling behind? How states include measures of 9th grade performance in their ESSA plans* [Brief]. Accessed at www.achieve.org/files/On-Track -Brief.pdf on April 24, 2024.

Advancement Project. (2014). *Restorative practices: Fostering healthy relationships & promoting positive discipline in schools.* Accessed at https://advancementproject.org /resources/restorative-practices-fostering-healthy-relationships-promoting-positive -discipline-in-schools on April 24, 2024.

Aguilar, E. (2020). *Coaching for equity: Conversations that change practice.* San Francisco: Jossey-Bass.

Anderson, A. (2017). *"It just weighs in the back of your mind": Microaggressions in science.* [Doctoral dissertation, DePaul University]. Digital Commons @ DePaul. Accessed at https://via.library.depaul.edu/csh_etd/203 on April 24, 2024.

Ansoff, H. I. (1957). Strategies for diversification. *Harvard Business Review, 35*(5), 113–124.

Ariely, D., Loewenstein, G., & Prelec, D. (2006). Tom Sawyer and the construction of value. In S. Lichtenstein & P. Slovic (Eds.), *The construction of preference* (pp. 271–281). Cambridge, UK: Cambridge University Press. https://doi .org/10.1017/cbo9780511618031.015

Arizona School Boards Association. (n.d.). *What is equity?* Accessed at https://azsba.org /about/equity/what-is-equity/#:~:text=Equal%20means%20%E2%80%9Csame %E2%80%9D%20whereas%20equity,at%20varying%20degrees%20of%20 readiness on August 6, 2024.

Ayuso, M., Bravo, J., & Holzmann, R. (2019). *Making use of home equity: The potential of housing wealth to enhance retirement security.* Accessed at www.iza.org/publications /dp/12656/making-use-of-home-equity-the-potential-of-housing-wealth-to-enhance -retirement-security on April 24, 2024.

Bailey, K. M., Curtis, A., & Nunan, D. (2001). *Pursuing professional development: The self as source.* Boston: Heinle & Heinle.

Baker, B., Farrie, D., & Sciarra, D. (2018). *Is school funding fair? A national report card* (7th ed.). Newark, NJ: Education Law Center. Accessed at https://eric.ed.gov /?id=ED584733#:~:text=Baker%2C%20Bruce%3B%20Farrie%2C%20Danielle %3B%20Sciarra%2C%20David%20G.&text=%22Is%20School%20Funding%20 Fair%3F,resources%20to%20the%20neediest%20students on April 24, 2024.

Baldwin, J. (1962). *As much truth as one can bear.* Accessed at https://timesmachine .nytimes.com/timesmachine/1962/01/14/issue.html on August 15, 2022.

Balfanz, R., & Byrnes, V. (2006). Closing the mathematics achievement gap in high-poverty middle schools: Enablers and constraints. *Journal of Education for Students Placed at Risk, 11*(2), 143–159. http://dx.doi.org/10.1207/s15327671espr1102_2

Banaji, M. R., & Greenwald, A. G. (1995). Implicit gender stereotyping in judgments of fame. *Journal of Personality and Social Psychology, 68*(2), 181–198.

Banaji, M. R., & Greenwald, A. G. (2013). *Blindspot: Hidden biases of good people.* New York: Delacorte Press.

Banerjee, A. V. (1992). A simple model of herd behavior. *Quarterly Journal of Economics, 107*(3), 797–817.

Banks, J. A., & McGee Banks, C. A. (2019). *Multicultural education: Issues and perspectives* (10th ed.). Hoboken, NJ: Wiley.

Baumeister, R. F. (1998). The self. In D. T. Gilbert, S. T. Fiske, & G. Lindzey (Eds.), *Handbook of social psychology* (4th ed., pp. 680–740). New York: McGraw Hill.

Baumeister, R. F., Bratslavsky, E., Muraven, M., & Tice, D. M. (1998). Ego depletion: Is the active self a limited resource? *Journal of Personality and Social Psychology, 74*(5), 1252–1265.

Baumeister, R. F., & Heatherton, T. F. (1996). Self-regulation failure: An overview. *Psychological Inquiry, 7*(1), 1–15.

Baumeister, R. F., & Tierney, J. (2011). *Willpower: Rediscovering the greatest human strength.* New York: Penguin.

Benson, B., Manoogian, J., III, & Wikipedia contributors. (2016). *Cognitive bias codex* [Infographic]. Accessed at www.sog.unc.edu/sites/www.sog.unc.edu/files/course _materials/Cognitive%20Biases%20Codex.pdf on April 24, 2024.

Berg, M. A., & Huang, J. (2015). Improving in-service teachers' effectiveness: K–12 academic literacy for the linguistically diverse. *Functional Linguistics, 2*(1), 1–21.

Berk, L. E. & Meyers, A. B. (2016). *Infants and children: Prenatal through middle childhood* (8th ed.). Boston: Pearson.

Bias. (n.d.) In *Merriam-Webster.com dictionary*. Accessed at www.merriam-webster.com /dictionary/bias on April 22, 2024.

Borrero N. E., & Bird S. L. (2009). *Closing the achievement gap: How to pinpoint student strengths to differentiate instruction and help your striving readers succeed.* New York: Scholastic.

Boysen, G. A., & Vogel, D. L. (2009). Bias in the classroom: Types, frequencies, and responses. *Teaching of Psychology, 36*(1): 12–17.

Brewer, M. B. (2007). The social psychology of intergroup relations: Social categorization, ingroup bias, and outgroup prejudice. In A. W. Kruglanski & E. T. Higgins (Eds.), *Social psychology: Handbook of basic principles* (2nd ed., pp. 695–715). New York: Guilford Press.

Brons, L. L. (2015). Othering, an analysis. *Transience a Journal of Global Studies, 6*(1), 69–90.

Brownlee, J. (2020). Cognitive shortcuts and public support for intervention. *Journal of Conflict Resolution, 64*(2–3), 261–289.

Carter, P. L. (2010). Race and cultural flexibility among students in different multiracial schools. *Teachers College Record, 112*(6), 1529–1574.

Centre for Evidence-Based Medicine & University of Oxford. (n.d.). *Catalogue of bias.* Accessed at https://catalogofbias.org on April 24, 2024.

Chapman, G. B., & Bornstein, B. H. (1996). The more you ask for, the more you get: Anchoring personal injury verdicts. *Applied Cognitive Psychology, 10*(6), 519–540. https://doi.org/10.1002/(sici)1099–0720(199612)10:6<519::aid-acp417>3.0.co;2–5

Council of Chief State School Officers. (2017). *Leading for equity: Opportunities for state education chiefs.* Accessed at https://ccsso.org/sites/default/files/2018-01/Leading%20 for%20Equity_011618.pdf on April 24, 2024.

Cialdini, R. B. (2007). *Influence: The psychology of persuasion* (Rev. ed.). New York: Collins.

Collado, W., Hollie, S., Isiah, R., & Jackson, Y. (2023). *Beyond conversations about race: A guide for discussions with students, teachers, and communities (how to talk about racism in schools and implement equitable classroom practices).* Bloomington, IN: Solution Tree Press.

Coopersmith, S. (1974). *The formative years: Principles of early childhood education.* Buffalo, NY: Albion Publishing Company.

DiAngelo, R. (2018). *White fragility: Why it's so hard for white people to talk about racism.* Boston: Beacon Press.

Dierenfield, B. (2007). *The battle over school prayer: Howe Engel v. Vitale Changed America.* Lawrence, KS: University Press of Kansas.

Diller, J. V., & Moule, J. (2005). *Cultural competence: A primer for educators.* Belmont, CA: Wadsworth.

Downey, D. B., & Pribesh, S. (2004). When race matters: Teachers' evaluations of students' classroom behavior. *Sociology of Education, 77*(4). 267–282. https://doi.org/10.1177/003804070407700401

Duckworth, A. (2016). *Grit: The power of passion and perseverance.* New York: Scribner.

DuFour, R., DuFour, R., Eaker, R., Many, T. W., Mattos, M., & Muhammad, A. (2024). *Learning by doing: A handbook for Professional Learning Communities at Work®* (4th ed.). Bloomington, IN: Solution Tree Press.

DuFour, R., Reeves, D., & DuFour, R. (2018). *Responding to the Every Student Succeeds Act with the PLC at Work process.* Bloomington, IN: Solution Tree Press.

Dweck, C. (2016). *Mindset: The new psychology of success* (2nd ed.). New York: Random House.

Eberhardt, J. L. (2020). *How racial bias works—And how to disrupt it* [Video]. TED Conferences. Accessed at www.ted.com/talks/jennifer_l_eberhardt_how_racial_bias_works_and_how_to_disrupt_it on April 24, 2024.

Education Plus®. (n.d.). Accessed at https://edplus.org on August 8, 2024.

Englich, B., & Soder, K. (2009). Moody experts—How mood and expertise influence judgmental anchoring. *Judgment and Decision Making, 4*(1), 41–50. https://doi.org/10.1017/S1930297500000693

Enough, B., & Mussweiler, T. (2001). Sentencing under uncertainty: Anchoring effects in the courtroom. *Journal of Applied Social Psychology, 31*(7), 1535–1551. https://doi.org/10.1111/j.1559–1816.2001.tb02687.x

Epley, N., & Gilovich, T. (2002). Putting adjustment back in the anchoring and adjustment heuristic. *Heuristics and Biases, 12*(5), 139–149. https://doi.org/10.1017/cbo9780511808098.009

Equal. (n.d.). In *Merriam-Webster.com dictionary.* Accessed at www.merriam-webster.com/dictionary/equality on August 4, 2024.

Equality. (n.d.). In *Merriam-Webster.com dictionary.* Accessed at www.merriam-webster.com/dictionary/equality on August 4, 2024.

Equity. (n.d.). In *Merriam-Webster.com dictionary.* Accessed at www.merriam-webster.com/dictionary/equity on April 24, 2024.

Erikson, E. H. (1994). *Identity and the life cycle.* New York: W.W. Norton & Company. Original work published 1959.

Feldman, D. H. (2003). Cognitive development in childhood. In R. M. Lerner, M. A. Easterbrooks, & J. Mistry (Eds.), *Handbook of psychology: Vol. 6, developmental psychology* (pp. 195–210). Hoboken, NJ: Wiley.

Fields, H. E., III. (2021). *Eazy-e: Oversimplifying equity and the harm it causes* [Webinar] Accessed at www.youtube.com/watch?v=-XvWhZqhAsI on July 12, 2022.

Fisher, D., Frey, N., & Almarode, J. (2019). 5 questions PLCs should ask to promote equity. *The Learning Professional, 40*(5), 44–47.

Fisher, D., Frey, N., Almarode, J., Flories, K., & Nagel, D. (2019). *The PLC+ playbook, grades K–12: A hands-on guide to collectively improving student learning.* Thousand Oaks, CA: Corwin Press.

Fiske, S. T. (1998) Stereotyping, prejudice, and discrimination. In Gilbert, D. T., Fiske, S. T., & Lindzey, G. (Eds.), *The handbook of social psychology* (4th ed., Vols. 1 and 2, pp. 357–411). New York: McGraw-Hill.

Fiske, S. T., & Taylor, S. E. (2013). *Social cognition: From brains to culture.* Thousand Oaks, CA: Sage.

Furnham, A., & Boo, H. C. (2011). A literature review of the anchoring bias. *Journal of Socio-Economics, 40*(1), 35–42.

Gallup. (2012, March). *Special report: 3.4% of U.S. adults identify as LGBT—Inaugural Gallup findings based on more than 120,000 interviews.* Accessed at https://news.gallup .com/poll/158066/special-report-adults-identify-lgbt.aspx on July 23, 2024.

Gallup. (2024, March). *LGBTQ+ identification in U.S. now at 7.6%.* Accessed at https:// news.gallup.com/poll/611864/lgbtq-identification.aspx on July 23, 2024.

Gladwell, M. (2005). *Blink: The power of thinking without thinking.* New York: Little, Brown and Company.

Goldberg, S. K., Rothblum, E. D., Russell, S. T., & Meyer, I. H. (2020). Exploring the Q in LGBTQ: Demographic characteristic and sexuality of queer people in a U.S. representative sample of sexual minorities. *Psychology of Sexual Orientation and Gender Diversity, 7*(1), 101–112. https://doi.org/10.1037/sgd0000359

Hamley, L., Houkamau, C. A., Osborne, D., Barlow, F. K., & Sibley, C. G. (2020). Ingroup love or outgroup hate (or both)? Mapping distinct bias profiles in the population. *Personality and Social Psychology Bulletin, 46*(2), 171–188. doi:10.1177/0146167219845919

Hart, B., & Risley, T. R. (1995). *Meaningful differences in the everyday experience of young American children.* Baltimore: Brookes Publishing.

Hattie, J. A. C. (2023). *Visible learning: The sequel—A synthesis of over 2,100 meta-analyses relating to achievement.* New York: Routledge.

Hess, F. M., & Eden, M. (2021). *The Every Student Succeeds Act (ESSA): What it means for schools, systems, and states.* Cambridge, MA: Harvard Education Press.

Hippocrates. (1868). *Hippocrates collected works* (W. H. S. Jones, Ed.). Cambridge: Harvard University Press. (Original work published ca. 400 B.C.E.)

Hollie, S. (2012). *Culturally and linguistically responsive teaching and learning: Classroom practices for student success.* Huntington Beach, CA: Shell Education.

Hollie, S. (2018). *Culturally and linguistically responsive teaching and learning: Classroom practices for student success* (2nd ed.). Huntington Beach, CA: Shell Education.

Hollie, S., & Muhammad, A. (2011). *The will to lead, the skill to teach: Transforming schools at every level.* Bloomington, IN: Solution Tree Press.

Human Rights Campaign. (2021). *We are here: LGBTQ+ adult population in United States reaches at least 20 million, according to Human Rights Campaign Foundation report.* Accessed at www.hrc.org/press-releases/we-are-here-lgbtq-adult-population-in-united-states-reaches-at-least-20-million-according-to-human-rights-campaign-foundation-report on August 8, 2024.

Illinois State Board of Education. (2022). *Equity information and resources.* Accessed at www.isbe.net/equity on July 19, 2024.

Janis, I. L. (1997). Groupthink. In R. P. Vecchio (Ed.), *Leadership: Understanding the dynamics of power and influence in organizations* (pp. 163–176). Notre Dame, IN: University of Notre Dame Press.

Jeffries, H. K. (2019). *Understanding and teaching the Civil Rights Movement* (The Harvard Goldberg Series for Understanding and Teaching History). Madison, Wisconsin: University of Wisconsin Press.

Kadlic, M., & Lesiak, M. A. (2003). *Early reading and scientifically-based research: Implications for practice in early childhood education programs* [Conference presentation]. National Association of State Title I Directors of Conference, Seattle, Washington.

Kahneman, D. (2011). *Thinking, fast and slow.* New York: Farrar, Straus and Giroux.

Kail, R. V., & Cavanaugh, J. C. (2019). *Human development: a life-span view* (8th ed.). Boston: Cengage Learning, Inc.

Kameda, T., Tsukasaki, T., Hastie, R., & Berg, N. (2011). Democracy under uncertainty: The wisdom of crowds and the free-rider problem in group decision making. *Psychological Review, 118*(1), 76–96.

Kameda, T., Wisdom, T., Toyokawa, W., & Inukai, K. (2012). Is consensus-seeking unique to humans? A selective review of animal group decision-making and its implications for (human) social psychology. *Group Processes and Intergroup Relations, 15*(5), 673–689.

Karade, B. I. (1994). *The handbook of Yoruba religious concepts.* Newburyport, MA: Weiser Books.

Kruger, J., & Dunning, D. (1999). Unskilled and unaware of it: How difficulties in recognizing one's own incompetence lead to inflated self-assessments. *Journal of Personality and Social Psychology, 77*(6), 1121–1134.

Kwon, W.-S., Deshpande, G., Katz, J., & Byun, S.-E. (2017). What does the brain tell about scarcity bias? Cognitive neuroscience evidence of decision making under scarcity. *International Textile and Apparel Association Annual Conference Proceedings, 74*(1). Accessed at www.iastatedigitalpress.com/itaa/article/1656/galley/1529/view on April 24, 2024.

Le Bon, G. (1895). *The crowd: A study of the popular mind.* Mineola, NY: Dover Publications.

LeDoux, J. E. (1998). *The emotional brain: The mysterious underpinnings of emotional life.* New York: Simon and Schuster.

Lee, C.-Y., & Morewedge, C. K. (2022). Noise increases anchoring effects. *Psychological Science, 33*(1), 60–75. Accessed at https://doi.org/10.1177/09567976211024254 on July 19, 2024.

Lindsey, R. B., Robins, K. N., & Terrell, R. D. (2003). *Cultural proficiency: A manual for school leaders* (2nd ed.). Thousand Oaks, CA: Corwin.

Lovallo, D., & Kahneman, D. (2003, July). Delusions of success: How optimism undermines executives' decisions. *Harvard Business Review.* Accessed at https://hbr.org/2003/07/delusions-of-success-how-optimism-undermines-executives-decisions on April 24, 2024.

Makari, G., (2021). *Of fear and strangers: A history of xenophobia.* New York: Norton.

Marchiori, D., Papies, E. K., & Klein, O. (2014). The portion size effect on food intake. An anchoring and adjustment process? *Appetite, 81,* 108–115. https://doi.org/10.1016/j.appet.2014.06.018

Maslow, A. H. (1943). A theory of human motivation. *Psychological Review, 50*(4), 370–396. https://doi.org/10.1037/h0054346

May, T., & Perry, B. (2011). *Social research and reflexivity: Content, context and consequences.* London: SAGE.

McKenzie, K. B., & Skrla, L. (2011). *Using equity audits in the classroom to reach and teach all students.* Thousand Oaks, CA: Corwin.

McNair, T. B., Bensimon, E. M., & Malcom-Piqueux, L. (2020). *From equity talk to equity walk: Expanding practitioner knowledge for racial justice in higher education.* San Francisco: Jossey-Bass.

Moore, A. (2007). *The South's tolerable alien: Roman Catholics in Alabama and Georgia, 1945–1970.* Baton Rouge, LA: Louisiana State University Press.

Muhammad, A. (2009). *Transforming school culture: How to overcome staff division.* Bloomington, IN: Solution Tree Press.

Muhammad, A., & Cruz, L. (2019). *Time for change: Four essential skills for transformational school and district leaders.* Bloomington, IN: Solution Tree Press.

Mussweiler, T., Strack, F., & Pfeiffer, T. (2000). Overcoming the inevitable anchoring effect: Considering the opposite compensates for selective accessibility. *Personality and Social Psychology Bulletin, 26*(9), 1142–1150.

National Center for Education Statistics. (2011). *The condition of education 2011.* Accessed at https://nces.ed.gov/pubs2011/2011033.pdf on November 15, 2022.

National Center for Education Statistics. (2012). *The condition of education 2012.* Accessed at https://nces.ed.gov/pubs2012/2012045.pdf on November 15, 2022

National Center for Education Statistics. (2013). *The condition of education 2013.* Accessed at https://nces.ed.gov/pubs2013/2013037.pdf on November 15, 2022.

National Center for Education Statistics. (2014). *The condition of education 2014.* Accessed at https://nces.ed.gov/pubs2014/2014083.pdf on November 15, 2022.

National Center for Education Statistics. (2024). *Students with disabilities.* Accessed at https://nces.ed.gov/programs/coe/indicator/cgg on July 28, 2024.

National Equity Project. (2024). *Educational equity means that each child receives what they need to develop to their full academic and social potential.* Accessed at www.nationalequityproject.org/education-equity-definition on July 19, 2024.

Neitzel, J., & Mead, E. (2023). *Inclusive practices in early childhood education.* Towson, MD: Brooks Publishing.

New York State Education Department. (n.d.). *Advancing educational equity.* Accessed at www.nysed.gov/essa/advancing-educational-equity on July 20, 2024.

Patterson, K., Grenny, J., McMillan, R., & Switzler, A. (2012). *Crucial conversations: Tools for talking when stakes are high* (2nd ed.). New York: McGraw Hill.

Perry, T., Zemelman, S., & Smith, K. A. (2022). *Teaching for racial equity: Becoming interrupters.* Portland, ME: Stenhouse Publishers.

Pew Research Center. (2020). *On the cusp of adulthood and facing an uncertain future: What we know about gen Z so far.* Accessed at www.pewresearch.org/social-trends /2020/05/14/on-the-cusp-of-adulthood-and-facing-an-uncertain-future-what-we -know-about-gen-z-so-far-2 on June 3, 2022.

Pierce, C. M., Carew, J. V., Pierce-Gonzalez, D., & Willis, D. (1978). An experiment in racism: TV commercials. In C. M. Pierce (Ed.), *Television and education* (pp. 62–88). Thousand Oaks, CA: Sage.

powell, j. a. (2006). *Talking the walk: A communications guide for racial justice.* Chico, CA: AK Press.

powell, j. a. (2015). *Racing to justice: Transforming our conceptions of self and other to build an inclusive society.* Bloomington, IN: Indiana University Press.

Recht, D. R., & Leslie, L. (1988). Effect of prior knowledge on good and poor readers' memory of text. *Journal of Educational Psychology, 80*(1), 16–20.

Saturday Night Live. (1982). *Black stereotype sketch* [Video]. Accessed at www.youtube .com/watch?v=BKPi66Us27Q on April 24, 2024.

Singleton, G. E. (2015). *Courageous conversations about race: A field guide for achieving equity in schools* (2nd ed.). Thousand Oaks, CA: Corwin.

Skiba, R. J., & Peterson, R. L. (2000). School discipline at a crossroads: From zero tolerance to early response. *Exceptional Children, 66*(3), 335–346. Accessed at https:// journals.sagepub.com/doi/abs/10.1177/001440290006600305#articleCitation DownloadContainer on April 24, 2024.

Skrla, L., McKenzie, K. B., & Scheurich, J. J. (2009). *Using equity audits to create equitable and excellent schools.* Thousand Oaks, CA: Corwin.

Smith, D., Frey, N., Pumpian, I., & Fisher, D. (2017). *Building equity: Policies and practices to empower all learners.* Arlington, VA: Association of Supervision and Development.

Spivak, G. C. (1985). The Rani of Sirmur: An essay in reading the archives. *History and Theory, 24*(3), 247–272.

Steele, C. (2011). *Whistling Vivaldi: How stereotypes affect us and what we can do.* New York: W.W. Norton & Company.

Stefanova, M. (2015). *Private equity accounting, investor reporting, and beyond.* Upper Saddle River, NJ: Pearson Education.

Strack, F., & Mussweiler, T. (1997). Explaining the enigmatic anchoring effect: Mechanisms of selective accessibility. *Journal of Personality and Social Psychology, 73*(3), 437–446. https://doi.org/10.1037/0022–3514.73.3.437

Sue, D. W. (2010). *Microaggressions in everyday life: Race, gender, and sexual orientation.* Hoboken, NJ: Wiley.

Sue, D. W., Bucceri, J., Lin, A. I., Nadal, K. L., & Torino, G. C. (2007). Racial microaggressions and the Asian American experience. *Cultural Diversity and Ethnic Minority Psychology, 13*(1), 72–81.

Sumner, W. G. (1906). *Folkways: A study of the sociological importance of usages, manners customs, mores, and morals.* Boston: Ginn and Company.

Sumner, W. G. (1911). *War and other essays.* New Haven, CT: Yale University Press.

Sumner, W. G. (1913). *Earth-hunger and other essays.* New Haven, CT: Yale University Press.

Sumner, W. G., Keller, A. G., & Davie, M. R. (1927). *The science of society.* New Haven, CT: Yale University Press.

Tajfel, H. (1982). Social psychology of intergroup relations. *Annual Review of Psychology, 33,* 1–39. https://doi.org/10.1146/annurev.ps.33.020182.000245

Tajfel, H., & Turner, J. C. (1986). The social identity theory of intergroup behavior. In W. G. Austin & S. Worchel (Eds.), *Psychology of intergroup relations* (2nd ed., pp. 7–24). Chicago: Nelson Hall.

Trotter, W. (1916). *Instincts of the herd in peace and war.* London: T. Fisher Unwin. https://doi.org/10.1037/13041–000

Tversky, A., & Kahneman, D. (1974). Judgment under uncertainty: Heuristics and biases. *Science, 185*(4157), 1124–1131. https://doi.org/10.21236/ad0767426

UNICEF. (2017). *Inclusive education: Including children with disabilities in quality learning—what needs to be done?* Accessed at www.unicef.org/eca/sites/unicef.org.eca/files/IE_summary_accessible_220917_brief.pdf on July 8, 2022.

University of Leeds. (2008, February 16). *Sheep in human clothing: Scientists reveal our flock mentality.* Accessed at www.sciencedaily.com/releases/2008/02/080214114517.htm on April 24, 2024.

U.S. Census Bureau. (n.d.). *Sexual orientation and gender identity (SOGI).* Accessed at www.census.gov/topics/population/sexual-orientation-gender-identity.html on June 6, 2023.

U.S. Census Bureau. (2010). *Overview of race and Hispanic origin: 2010.* Accessed at www.census.gov/library/publications/2011/dec/c2010br-02.html on June 1, 2023.

U.S. Census Bureau. (2020). *Measuring racial and ethnic diversity for the 2020 census.* Accessed at www.census.gov/newsroom/blogs/random-samplings/2021/08/measuring-racial-ethnic-diversity-2020-census.html on June 1, 2023.

U.S. Census Bureau. (2021). *U.S. population more racially and ethnically diverse than measured in 2010.* Accessed at www.census.gov/library/stories/2021/08/2020-united-states-population-more-racially-ethnically-diverse-than-2010.html on June 1, 2023.

U.S. Department of Education. (2015). *Every Student Succeeds Act (ESSA)*. Accessed at www.ed.gov/essa?src=rn on July 8, 2022.

Van Nunspeet, F., Ellemers, N., & Derks, B. (2015). Reducing implicit bias: How moral motivation helps people refrain from making "automatic" prejudiced associations. *Translational Issues in Psychological Science, 1*(4), 382–391.

Verkuyten, M. (2021). Group identity and ingroup bias: The social identity approach. *Human Development, 65* (5–6), 311–324. Accessed at https://karger.com/hde /article/65/5–6/311/828433/Group-Identity-and-Ingroup-Bias-The-Social on April 23, 2024.

Von Hecker, U., Klauer, K. C., & Aßfalg, A. (2019). A robust anchoring effect in linear ordering. *Quarterly Journal of Experimental Psychology, 72*(11). https://doi .org/10.1177/1747021819855234

Weinberg, G., & McCann, L. (2019). *Super thinking: The big book of mental models.* New York: Portfolio.

Winters, M.-F. (2013). From diversity to inclusion: An inclusion equation. In B. M. Ferdman & B. R. Deane (Eds.), *Diversity at work: The practice of inclusion* (pp. 205–228). 10.1002/9781118764282.ch7

Worchel, S., Lee, J., & Adewole, A. (1975). Effects of supply and demand on ratings of object value. *Journal of Personality and Social Psychology, 32*(5), 906–914.

Zenko, M. (2018, October 19). *Leaders can make dumb decisions. This exercise can fix that.* Accessed at https://fortune.com/2018/10/19/red-teams-decision-making-leadership on April 24, 2024.

Zhou, Y., & Shen, L. (2021). Confirmation bias and the persistence of misinformation on climate change. *Communication Research, 49*(4), 500–523. https://doi.org/10.1177 /00936502211028049

Zhu, M., & Ratner, R. K. (2015). Scarcity polarizes preferences: The impact on choice among multiple items in a product class. *Journal of Marketing Research, 52*(1), 13–26. https://doi.org/10.1509/jmr.13.0451

Zong, Y., & Guo, X. (2022). An experimental study on anchoring effect of consumers' price judgment based on consumers' experiencing scenes. *Frontiers in Psychology, 13.* https://doi.org/10.3389/fpsyg.2022.794135

# Index

## Finding Your Blind Spots

*Hedreich Nichols*

Author Hedreich Nichols infuses this book with a direct yet conversational style to help you identify biases that adversely affect your practice and learn how to move beyond those biases to ensure a more equitable, inclusive campus culture.
BKG022

## Transforming School Culture

*Anthony Muhammad*

This second edition provides a school improvement plan for leaders to overcome staff division, improve relationships, and build positive school cultures. Learn school leadership techniques for addressing the four types of teachers that impact your school culture.
BKF793

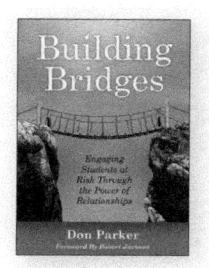

## Building Bridges

*Don Parker*

Research shows that discipline problems are one of the greatest challenges in education. In *Building Bridges*, author Don Parker shows educators how to address this issue head-on, to build teacher-student relationships and create a welcoming learning environment that promotes engagement and achievement.
BKF846

## A Blueprint for Belonging

*Morgane Michael*

Using this timely, research-based guide, educators can address challenging (but rewarding) social-emotional dynamics to help their school or district thrive. These proven, practical strategies and actionable steps help set the foundation for an inclusive, positive, and restorative community.
BKG185

# Wait! Your professional development journey doesn't have to end with the last pages of this book.

We realize improving student learning doesn't happen overnight. And your school or district shouldn't be left to puzzle out all the details of this process alone.

**No matter where you are on the journey, we're committed to helping you get to the next stage.**

Take advantage of everything from **custom workshops** to **keynote presentations** and **interactive web and video conferencing**. We can even help you develop an action plan tailored to fit your specific needs.

*Let's get the conversation started.*

Call 888.763.9045 today.

SolutionTree.com